DRESSAGE
ESSENTIALS

DRESSAGE
ESSENTIALS

JANE KIDD

HOWELL
BOOK HOUSE
New York

Howell Book House
A Simon & Schuster Macmillan Company
1633 Broadway
New York, NY 10019

MACMILLAN is a registered trademark of Macmillan, Inc.

Library of Congress Cataloguing-in-Publication Data

Kidd, Jane.
    Dressage essentials / Jane Kidd.
        p.   cm.
    Includes index.
    ISBN 1-58245-001-3
    1. Dressage.   I. Title
    SF309.5.K524   1999
    798.2 ' 3--dc21   98-34967
                                                  CIP

ISBN: 1-58245-001-3

10 9 8 7 6 5 4 3 2

Printed in Italy

Contents

Foreword

Many people find dressage confusing and complicated. As a professional writer who also rides, judges and trains I hope I can make a contribution by simplifying it, even if it is at the expense of covering all possibilities and examining the subject in the depth that the maestros themselves have done.

To me, the important factor is that riders, judges and spectators can be helped to grasp the 'basics', to understand the foundations of the sport without being put off by the detail, esoteric ideas and contingencies which will become intelligible as more is learnt about the fascinating art of dressage. The foundations are the basis of the art, and all too often they are skipped over in an eagerness to get to the more advanced work. The problem is that if they are not understood and incorporated as part of the training, then the horse will find it difficult to learn and the rider to master the more complicated aspects of dressage.

Establishing the foundations is fascinating in itself, and the tendency to overlook them has been a major handicap amongst the

nations who lack a long tradition of dressage, mainly the English-speaking countries. I hope this book will make some contribution towards giving participators and onlookers a clearer idea about the concepts they need to understand before advancing, and will have to keep returning to even in the highest echelons of dressage. I hope it will also provide clear information about the more basic movements that can help to develop those foundations. Any simplification is purely in the interests of keeping the text clear and concise enough to achieve my aim of making dressage more understandable.

I would like to thank the many people who have helped me, the trainers and riders who have given me inspiration and ideas, and the riders who have acted as guinea pigs for the pictures and who, in order to help other people to learn, are not always shown at their best.

The Horse

T he bible for dressage competitors and judges, the FEI rule book, lays down that:

The object of dressage is the harmonious development of the physique and ability of the horse. As a result it makes the horse calm, supple, loose and flexible, but also confident, attentive and keen, thus achieving perfect understanding with his rider.

The tests of these qualities are:

1 free, regular paces,
2 harmony, lightness and ease in all movements,
3 impulsion with engagement of the hindquarters, and a lightening of the forehand, and
4 acceptance of the bridle without tension or resistance, so there is submission throughout the body.

A dressage horse therefore needs paces which are naturally athletic, and correct (see chapter 4), a character which will accept and enjoy the work so he does it willingly and not dourly, and a conformation that will help him keep his balance so he can move lightly and without resistance and which enables him to develop the crucial power in his hindquarters and lightness in his forehand.

Dressage horses do come in all shapes and sizes; from the USA a 14.2hh Connemara pony, Seldom Seen, was one of the best Grand Prix horses; from Switzerland, the great horse from 1976–82, the World, European and Olympic champion Granat was a big, hefty, old-fashioned Holstein, whereas from Germany the 1988 and 1992 Olympic champion Rembrandt is more of a Thoroughbred type. Although the trend is towards a lighter, more elegant horse, the important factor is not the type, but that the horse is an athlete with the make and shape and character to make it easy to maintain, develop and control that athleticism.

CONFORMATION

OVERALL IMPRESSION

Although paces are the crucial natural asset in a dressage horse, a big free-moving horse is a very risky proposition if weaknesses in conformation mean he is liable to unsoundness or difficulties in producing impulsion, acceptance of the bridle, harmony, and lightness in his work.

By far the most important aspect of conformation in a dressage horse is the balance and homogeneity of its overall make and shape. Just like in the riding, the impression must be of harmony with the forehand balancing the hindquarters. A powerful hindquarters is of no value if the forehand is weak, a big head will be unbalancing on a short thin neck. There must be an impression of equilibrium and it is better to have all sectors of a uniform, if slightly lower standard, then one sector very strong and another very weak.

The natural ability of a horse – his paces – can only be maintained and developed when he is in balance and it takes tremendous skill to balance a horse whose conformation is not well proportioned.

THE HEAD

Heads of dressage horses vary from small pony-like ones to large ones with Roman noses. Apart from the need for the size to be in harmony with the rest of the body, the important factor is that the prospective rider likes it. The head is one of the most important indicators of character. Some like small pretty heads which are usually found on quick-minded horses, others the bigger, more common heads which are associated with wiser and slower-thinking horses.

Useful indicators of character are the ears. When these are small and turned in at the top the horse is usually sharp and not too generous; when they are big and broad at the base the character is kinder. The way they move is also important – if they are twitchy, move quickly, and often go back this is a

A balanced conformation helps to produce a balanced way of going

A head that indicates an intelligent and alert character

sign of a suspicious character. If often held forward and moved more purposefully then it is a sign of a bolder, more thoughtful horse.

Eyes, too, give away much about the character both in shape and the way they move. Large round dark ones indicate a good bold character. Small, quick-moving ones that are often glancing backwards belong to more wary characters. Some riders do not like white around the eye, as it is often associated with a difficult character. A surer sign of difficulties ahead for the rider in achieving harmony with the horse's character is a small bump in the skull just above and between the eyes.

The shape of the head, the ears and eyes are the character indicators. The mouth is important because it is where the bit goes. Deficiencies like parrot mouths cause few problems, other than sometimes making it difficult to keep a horse with one looking well; they find it more difficult to eat. What is important is that a bit can fit into the mouth easily and comfortably; a small short mouth can be a difficult basis for the double bridle. Inside the mouth, check for any signs of damage that cannot be corrected, or skin infections or allergies. Ask your vet if you are worried.

The mouth has much to do with whether the horse will learn to accept the bit happily and without resistance, but so too does the manner in which the head articulates with the neck. The head must be mobile if the horse is to be able to flex and come onto the bit. This means that heads that appear as an extension out of a short thick-set neck, are to be avoided. A clearly defined, mobile area of articulation is needed and with minimal interference to flexion.

To provide the freedom to flex, the lower jaw bones should not be too deep (horizontally) otherwise they will press against the neck, restricting movement and causing pain when flexing. Nor should the jowl (the area between the lower jaw and the muscles of the vertebrae) be too thick as this would again restrict the ability to flex.

The flexion should originate at the poll and not further down the neck which is the case in what is known as a 'broken-necked' horse. To facilitate this crucial flexion at the poll, the area which covers the atlas, the universal joint, should be broad and long so there is space, and a good base, for mobility.

THE NECK

The neck helps the horse to keep his balance. When it is relatively long it is difficult to stabilise and therefore to keep the horse balanced. A shorter neck goes with a more balanced horse, but its greater stability often leads to fixing of the muscles and difficulties in maintaining looseness.

Ideally the shape should be convex along the top line, and concave or straight underneath. A ewe neck (concave on top) is associated with a stiff hollow back, and difficulties in getting the horse to soften and come onto the bit. It is possible for a skilled rider to improve the shape of the neck in a young horse.

Just as with the head and even more important

than the shape, is how the neck is set onto the next part of the body, the wither and shoulder. The join at the withers should be a firm, pliant one; horses which are very loose at the wither use this area like a hinge joint, bending the neck without the rest of their body. This makes it difficult to keep them straight and balanced.

Ideally the neck should grow out of the top of the withers at right angles to the shoulders as this will make it much easier to lighten the forehand, than if the neck is set on lower, with its highest point below the withers.

THE SHOULDERS

Everybody looks for a long sloping shoulder as this gives more spring and freedom to the strides, but it is as important to have a deep shoulder as one that is set at a distinct angle. The shoulder also affects another crucial factor, the saddle position. In dressage it is important for the rider to be positioned well back and not over the shoulders, as an aim of training is to gradually transfer the weight the horse carries backwards off the forehand towards the hindquarters. This will help the horse to become lighter and more mobile when he carries the rider.

THE WITHER

The wither affects this saddle position and the longer and higher it is the more it will help to stabilise the saddle position further back. The length is more important than the height and an excessively high wither can make it difficult to fit a saddle. Short flat withers with upright shallow shoulders are to be avoided as the saddle tends to slip forward over the top of them, putting more of the weight on to the forehand.

THE ELBOWS

The elbows are another indicator of the degree of freedom of movement. If 'tied in' ie they turn inwards so that the limbs tend to splay outwards, then the action will be restricted and often clumsy. The other extreme, when the point far out, can also cause problems as the horse will tend to be pigeon toed ie the feet turned inwards and on a narrower base than the top of the limbs.

THE FORELEGS

Any deviation of the limbs from the vertical line – forwards, backwards or to either side – will not only mean that more strain is put on one area than another, making the horse more liable to soundness problems, but will also affect the freedom of movement.

An important role of the forelimbs is to be strong enough to take the considerable strain of working for and under the weight of the rider. The dressage horse tends to have more joint than tendon problems and any lack of clear definition, and the presence of swellings or bumps, indicate a possibility of future problems. The 'bone' circumference below the knee should be sufficient for the limbs to carry the body with ease, ie limbs not too thin. The pasterns ideally should slope at about 45 degrees as if more they tend to place extra strain on the tendons, if less they cannot act as such good shock absorbers, making the horse's movement more rigid and putting the joints at risk.

THE FEET

The front feet are also an area of weakness, with foot problems being an all-too-common reason for the end of a promising dressage horse's career, or at least a cause for shortening and stiffening of the strides. Good resilient horn is needed and the feet open and rounded with plenty of depth at the heels. The crucial factor is that the feet are balanced. This means that firstly, each pair (front and hind) has feet of the same size; that secondly, when viewed from in front a vertical line through the centre divides each foot into two equal halves; and that thirdly, when viewed from the side the pastern continues into the foot with no break, so there is no angle at the coronet, and the foot/pastern axis is straight. The heels of each foot should be well apart with no tendency to contract. A good blacksmith can do much to ease or correct these problems, especially with a young horse, but if they are noted in a possible purchase it is best to consider X-rays to ensure they have not already led to problems inside the feet.

THE BACK

The short-backed horse is usually easier to collect and keep between the leg and hand, but like the short neck, the muscles tend to set and stiffen. Such a horse is difficult to keep loose, which is not the case for a long-backed version, provided it is well muscled. The problem in the latter case is that it is more difficult for the hind legs to step under the weight, and in the walk such a horse often cannot overtrack. The ideal is between these two extremes.

Backs that are convex (roach) or concave (sway) are weaker and therefore a horse with either will find it difficult to work with elasticity, swing and engagement.

THE HINDQUARTERS

These are the source of power and should not be higher (except in a horse which is growing) than the withers. If the horse is croup high then the power from the hindquarters is directed down onto the forehand rather than up to it. This will make it difficult to get the weight off the forehand which will make training very difficult and put great strain on the forelegs.

As the horse's source of power, the hindquarters need to be broad and deep to provide plenty of muscle area. A rounded shape to the croup is favoured – if flat, it is difficult to bring the hind legs under the body, and if sheet, the hinds come under with such ease that their flexibility is restricted. The important factors are that the hip joint is low (easiest to locate when the horse walks) and the stifle well forward, as these, together with a long and muscular upper thigh, provide the propulsive power for the horse to step under and build up impulsion.

HIND LEGS

As for the forelimbs, the posture of the hind limbs is important. If when viewed from the rear the hocks turn in (cow hocks) or out (bowed hocks), strength is lost and extra strain is put on these important lever joints. From the side a straight vertical line from the point of the buttock should just touch the back of the hock and fetlock, and limbs which deviate either side of this are rarely so strong or so able to remain flexible and/or bring the hind legs further under the weight of the body.

There will be many examples of successful horses who do not conform to these points and no horse will conform to them all. The perfect horse does not exist, and at best it is a matter of hoping that one weakness will be offset by another strong point. The most important point to look for in a dressage horse is the overall balance and harmony, and the areas which appear to have most effect on his future in this field are the power of the hindquarters, the saddle position and the way the neck and the head are set on to the withers and neck respectively.

Conformation is, however, only one aspect of a dressage horse. Character is very important, and this is much more difficult to assess.

CHARACTER

The character is much more of a personal preference than the conformation. Each person finds it easier to understand and communicate with certain types. The sensitive rider may like a nervous horse which needs to be given confidence; the bold rider might enjoy the challenge of an obstreperous, wilful or high-spirited type; the nervous rider a horse which is 'laid back' and not too anxious; the clumsy rider a lazy horse; and the refined rider a very sensitive one. The important factor for any dressage horse is that he is bold, and enjoys work.

The character assessment starts with the head, and as already discussed, the eyes and ears are good indicators. When testing the horse, constantly monitor how he reacts to circumstances and commands; try testing his boldness by facing him with some new surroundings/obstacle or aids. Test his keenness to work by returning to the stables and then taking him out again. Handle him in the stable and/or the field – although take into account his age, background, how well he has been trained and his history.

The layman's view of a dressage horse tends to be that he is obedient and subservient. In practice, however, one that goes methodically through the movements showing no presence or spirit might be a good schoolmaster but becomes pretty dull to ride, and in the arena is rarely awarded high marks. Dressage is not subservience, but harmony between horse and rider. Most of the top horses have a touch of mischievousness that when controlled and directed, turns them into horses which really try for their riders, rather than being dour slaves.

SEX

The sex of the horse has a considerable effect on character. Geldings are the most popular for dressage as they tend to be the most co-operative and sensi-

ble. Mares and stallions both need people with special assets to handle and get the best out of them. Many people will not touch a mare as they are temperamental, often difficult when they come into season, and all too easily become obstinate and refuse to work. On the other hand, riders who understand the minds of mares find they try much harder, are much bolder than geldings and a large number have become top dressage performers.

Mares react to logical sensitive trainers who persuade them what should be done, and usually rebel or sulk if strong or clumsy riders try to use force.

Stallions are more popular than mares in dressage as they have that wonderful mark-earner – presence. Their necks are crested and they have

Carl Hester on Giorgione at Goodwood 1993 – a good type of stallion

such proud carriage that the eye is drawn towards them. They are also strong and intelligent. Their handlers and riders need to earn their respect through being very clear as to what is required, and quick to reprimand and reward as necessary, and then these intelligent creatures learn to trust and enjoy complying. Stallions are quick to recognise when a rider or handler is frightened or unsure, and are not horses for the inexperienced, especially when young.

BREEDS

In Europe breeders have been specifically producing horses which have the assets needed in dressage horses. The Hanoverian, Westphalian, Trakehner and Holstein in Germany, the Swedish, Danish, Dutch and Belgian Warmbloods, and the Selle Française have been specifically bred to have free, elastic paces, manageable characters and balanced conformation, in the same way as Thoroughbreds are bred to gallop

An International champion in young horse classes – Duvalier who is a Hanoverian with an excellent 'uphill' make and shape

as fast as possible. The result is that warmbloods are by far the most popular breeds of dressage horse.

The Thoroughbred, and cross-breds from Ireland, USA, UK and the Antipodes have not been scientifically produced for this sport. Some do have the right assets – Keen from the USA was a wonderfully talented Thoroughbred, as was Wily Trout who was a runner-up in the World Cup and Arak who qualified for the 1997 World Cup. Most top riders love Thoroughbreds. The difficulty is finding one with the paces, conformation and character, and who is not worth a fortune as a racehorse. Most breeds of horse are represented in dressage but the warmbloods are the breeds specifically bred for this market.

THE PACES

The paces are the horse's natural talent which the dressage training should maintain and develop. The aim is to harness that exciting ability to dance in the air when out in the field, to hardly touch the ground at trot, to bound into the air each stride at the canter, and swing loosely along when relaxed at the walk. The horse has to learn to balance himself with the rider on his back, and develop his physique so that he can at the rider's command willingly move in the way seen when free. The horse's ability as a dressage horse will be limited by his own natural ability to move when free. It is very difficult for a rider to improve a horse's natural paces, and more difficult to improve the walk and canter than the trot.

The qualification to this is that the horse's limitations may be due to physical problems – bad shoeing, bad riding, or hard ground. When assessing a horse try to give him the best possible chance to show off his ability himself by turning him loose on good going.

AT THE CANTER he should bound into the air each stride showing a clear three-time beat with a moment of suspension. The hocks should flex and not remain straight, and the direction of the movement should be upwards so his forehand lifts higher than the hindquarters, but without stiffening and hollowing his back.

Above: A good 'uphill' bounding canter

Right: A trot showing the joints of the limbs well flexed

AT THE TROT he should take light, elastic, rounded strides, moving fluently from one pair of diagonals to the other with a clear moment of suspension in between. His joints should flex so there is no flicking of the forelegs or dragging of the hinds.

AT THE WALK he should show that he can take purposeful long, free strides with his tail swinging slightly from one side to the other; this shows he is using the muscles in his back. Each hind foot should be put down well in front of the print of the fore-foot on the same side (overtracking). If the horse is excitable it can be difficult to appreciate the walk

A horse in a free rein walk who appears to be taking purposeful free strides

when free, and this is one pace which can be better assessed when led.

The walk should be a marching pace with a clear four-time beat. Some horses are born with a propensity towards a two-time walk and this will lose many marks in the arena.

The natural elasticity and spring to the paces is best assessed without a rider on the horse's back so if difficult to turn loose, try lungeing.

THE STRAIGHTNESS OF THE MOVEMENT

At the walk and trot this is best assessed when the horse is led in hand on a level, hard surface. He can be inspected first at the walk and then at the trot, coming towards and going away from the assessor. Ideally the limbs should move straight, neither brushing the side/s of the other leg/s nor swinging outwards. Any deviations affect balance, put more strain onto certain areas than others and can lead

to the horse hitting one leg with another. Very few horses move absolutely straight, especially the big elastic movers, as for them any slight swing is accentuated. The important factor is to assess the severity of the swing – and it is more unbalancing if just one of the fores or the hinds is affected – and look into the chances of improving it with good shoeing, or using boots or bandages.

For all but the very young horse it is important to see how the paces are affected by the weight of the rider. The walk should remain in the correct sequence (see chapter 4), the trot retain spring – although most trainers believe this is the easiest pace to improve – and the canter the balance, spring and clear three-time beat. An untrained horse finds it most difficult to establish balance in the canter, so allowance must be made for this.

The way a horse jumps will give an insight into his character and athleticism. Judge his boldness by the

Being run up to test for straight movement at the trot. This horse shows no tendency to swing the forelegs inwards or outwards

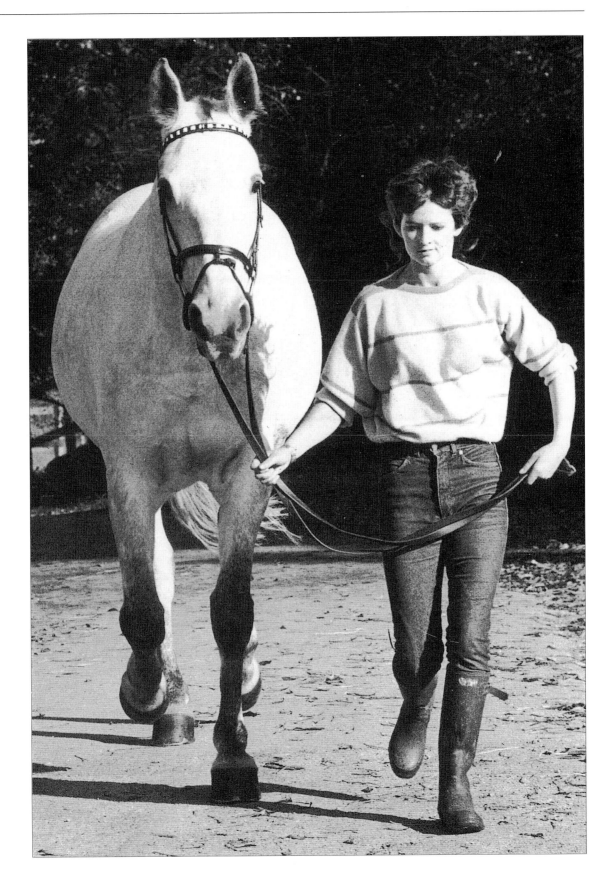

way he approaches; his lightness and agility, and the way he uses his back and neck by his style in the air.

No horse will go through this assessment with anywhere near 100% credits. The horse I brought on to Grand Prix had such a short walk he never over-tracked, and at the canter when free usually went into four-time and was often disunited. These were major debits, and there were many more on his conformation, but he was athletic, had presence and a reasonably balanced conformation. The important point is to keep in mind the goals of dressage as discussed on p26 and to assess how severe a handicap each deficit is likely to be, if it can be offset by other assets and whether it can be improved by training/shoeing/skilful care in the stable.

The other crucial point is to use instinct as well as logic. Do not talk yourself into liking a horse on that initial impression; the empathy – or lack of it – felt when first seeing and riding him is one of the best indicators as to whether you can train that horse to do dressage.

SOUNDNESS

However able the horse, however well the rider gets on with him, he is of no value in dressage if he goes lame. Gambles can be taken with horses that have weaknesses in wind, sight or heart, but a dressage horse's physique needs to be tough and supple.

Tendons do not have to stand up to so much as racehorses and eventers, but hocks, backs, joints and feet need to be particularly robust. A veterinary examination is always advisable as it is one of the worst disappointments to spend a lengthy time on training, and develop a good deal of affection and harmony only for the partnership to be ended by the exposure or worsening of a physical weakness.

SPECIAL CARE IN THE STABLE

Dressage horses are looked after in much the same way as other horses, but there are some areas of specialist care.

FEEDING

A dressage horse is fed so he looks well, not so lean as a racehorse, nor so fat as a show horse. He is also fed so that his rider can control him. One of the basics of dressage is impulsion (controlled forward momentum). That forwardness is vital, and hard feed can help to give him the energy to develop it, but not so much that he is out of control. How much energy is needed will depend largely on the rider. Top dressage riders like plenty of it as they are skilful enough to be able to direct and control it, but it could well end a novice rider's aspiration in dressage if the horse frightens him through misbehaviour and/or makes his hands very tough and strong by always pulling to go forwards.

Some horses with novice riders might need little more than grass and horse and pony cubes, whereas rather lazy horses with experienced riders might need 12–14lb (5.4–6.3kg) oats per day. Adjust the feeding so the horse has a good covering of flesh and muscles (able to feel but not see his ribs), enough energy to want to go forward, but not so much that he cannot be controlled.

AFTER WORK

With the concentrated work in an arena, dressage horses tend to sweat a good deal. It is important they are not returned to their stable/field hot and sticky as amongst other problems, this is likely to have adverse effects on those muscles that need to be kept so loose and supple. Most riders walk their horse until dry, but occasionally on a warm day it is a good idea to wash him down with tepid water, put on a cooler (sweat-rug) and keep him moving until he is dry.

Whether washed or walked until dry it is crucial that all sweat is removed, and this applies particularly to the saddle area. In dressage this is subjected to more pressure than other forms of riding and it is very easy for sores and bumps to develop. After dismounting, ease the girths but leave the saddle on for a few minutes; this does not then give such a sharp contrast in temperature and pressure to the saddle area. When the saddle is taken off, sponge the area thoroughly with warm water and rub dry to ensure it is clean and that circulation is stimulated. Feet and legs should receive plenty of attention, as in all good stable management.

Make sure the horse is kept warm after work. Dressage horses do not have to stand up to big temperature changes so it is quite acceptable to coddle them, to keep them in well protected stables and to use enough rugs to keep them warm (without sweating). Avoid letting them get cold because of the stiffening effects.

PREVENTIVE MEASURES

Dressage horses do not have to stand the strain of galloping across hard ground, but they do have to retain elasticity and spring to their paces. This is quickly lost if they are worked on hard surfaces, trotted on hard roads and if there is any soreness in the back, joints or feet.

THE FEET need daily attention to keep them free from stones and gravel which could cause problems, and oiled to keep the hoof wall in good condition. The important person is the blacksmith who must come regularly (at least every six weeks), and be skilled enough to balance the foot laterally and medially and allow enough room for the heels to grow and to avoid any contraction. Many problems have developed in dressage horses because they have been shod with long toes (a broken toe/pastern axis) and low and narrow at the heels.

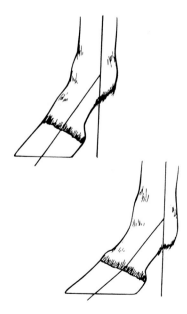

Correct (top) and a broken toe/pastern axis

JOINTS, particularly the hind fetlocks, tend to develop windgalls. Although unlikely to cause lameness, they will in the long run restrict mobility and it is best to stop them getting too numerous and large. Witch-hazel can be rubbed on occasionally and stable bandages (over gamgee or fibagee) worn at night.

If there are any signs of thickening in the hock or tendon areas then it is best to refer to a vet. If caught early problems in these vulnerable regions may never become serious.

THE BACK is a very difficult area to keep mobile and strong. Obviously it helps to have good training, a rider with a balanced seat, and a saddle that fits well (clears the withers and the spine easily and with panels that rest surely on the horse). The flatter type of saddle that spreads the load more evenly over the horse's back is more comfortable for the horse than the deep-seated version.

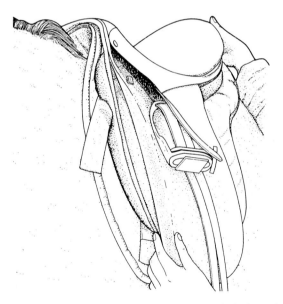

To avoid back problems, a well-fitted saddle, which clears the withers and spine is essential

If the horse dips when the rider gets on, if he swishes his tail when the rider sits positively into the saddle, or if the paces deteriorate, if he appears uncomfortable, then the back should be checked. Anybody can run his fingers along either side of the spine to see if this causes flinching in an area, but in

A dressage saddle that sits well on the horse's back. It is not too deep and the weight of the rider should be spread over a reasonably large surface area

Horses, like human athletes, benefit from physiotherapy, and one of the easiest for the amateur to use is the faradic machine

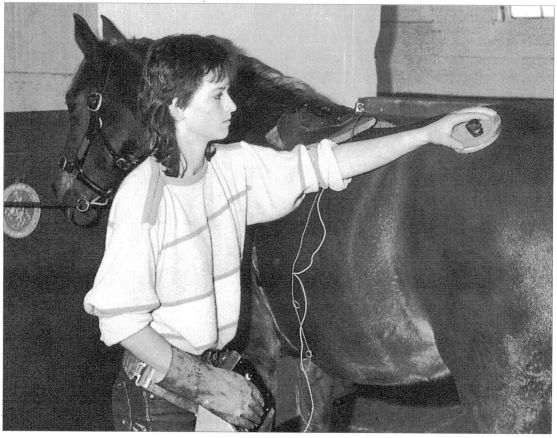

most cases it takes experience and skill to localise and identify a problem.

Vets will advise, and there are an increasing number of physiotherapists but these should only do the work if a vet refers a case to them. There are a host of machines (ultra sound, faradic, lasers etc) which can help in some cases. Most can be bought by anybody but expert advice is needed before using them. In the hands of a layman the faradic machine is probably the safest and most useful means of dealing with small problems and keeping the muscles supple.

Plenty of forms of alternative medicine are being used with horses from spiritual healers, to radionics to acupuncture to homoeopathy. When a talented and much loved horse starts to lose his gymnastic ability and if orthodox medicine is seen to be ineffective, then as long as the treatment can be afforded and the practitioner of it has good credentials, it is worth trying.

Before spending much money on remedial treatment, check out the training, as a bored or overworked horse can become listless and lethargic, and his cure would be variety, a holiday, more canters and jumping. A badly ridden horse can become unlevel or stiff: his cure is more training for the rider to sit in a balanced straight position; being ridden by someone else for short periods; and work on the lunge.

In keeping the horse sound and healthy, the most important factor to remember is that preventive medicine is the cheapest and most effective. To this end a dressage horse needs good thoughtful training, good daily aftercare in the stables (grooming, feeding and so on) and alertness as to potential problems (an ill-fitting saddle, a swelling appropriately and quickly treated).

2

The Rider

Almost any rider can do a dressage test. All that is required in the preliminary stages is to make the horse walk, trot, canter and stop, so it is not too difficult to complete the movements on a reasonably obliging horse. The skill, however, is not in completing the movement but in the way in which it is done. To do it well involves controlling and developing the horse's natural athleticism, to bring out his natural talents and not to stifle them in order to achieve obedience. This is not so easy, and it takes experience and hard work by the rider who should concentrate on the following:

1 Goals – to have very clear ideas as to what he is trying to achieve.
2 To stay in balance with the horse – to have a straight, upright, but relaxed position that will not interfere with the horse's balance.
3 Feel' – to know what the horse is doing and is about to do.
4 Communication – to develop a language that the horse understands ie the aids.
5 Physical fitness – to be fit enough to control the horse with ease.
6 Mental approach – to be able to concentrate without stiffening, to establish relaxed concentration, and be focused.

THE GOALS

Dressage can be a very complicated subject. There are numerous different techniques, styles and methods of achieving the movements. For the beginner this can be extremely confusing and for any rider, whatever his standard, losing sight of the objectives, thinking too much of how to do a movement, is likely to reduce the quality of the work. It is therefore very important for a rider to watch as much dressage as possible, and to decide what he likes, how he wants his horse to go. He should study the qualities in a good walk, trot, and canter; know what they look like, and better still, how they feel. Access to a good schoolmaster, or the chance to ride a good horse helps enormously in the development of clear goals.

For all the movements a rider must find out what a good shoulder in, half pass, transition and so on look and feel like, and keep them clearly in his mind as his goals.

Knowing what you want to achieve is a tremendous aid in achieving it. Although it is necessary to learn the techniques of how to do a movement these must never become so important that a clear picture of the goals is lost.

These goals, too, should be positive ones. Although it is useful to study faults – bad trots, canters, shoulders in etc – what to avoid should be secondary in the mind to what should be achieved. The successful dressage riders are those who think what should happen, not those who think what should not happen.

One of the best aspects of dressage is that so many standards of riders can enjoy it. The same sense of achievement can be felt by a disabled rider who gets his pony to do a good halt, as a top rider gets from a good piaffe

TO STAY IN BALANCE

The single most important prerequisite of a good dressage rider is a good position, although this is not an absolute, clearly defined position but one in which the rider stays in balance with the horse. At all times he must remain upright over the horse. If he deviates from a perpendicular line, above his horse, then he will have to hold himself by tensing his muscles, and his weight is unlikely to be distributed evenly thus forcing the horse into unequal use of the muscles. This will make it difficult for the horse to work correctly.

Some riders are able to stay in balance with rounded backs, with hollow backs, without maintaining a straight line from the shoulder through the hips to the heel, but for most it is easier to remain in balance from this basic position. The important factor is to maintain the position but without tension so it is not at the expense of the letting go of the muscles.

There are riders who sit upright, keep their heels down and look very correct, but are unable to get their horses to work correctly. They are either passengers or maintain their position through stiffness which inhibits the horse's action.

The FEI definition of the position of the rider does not fix the exact shape:

- All the movements should be obtained without apparent effort of the rider.
- He should be well balanced with his loins and hips supple, thighs and legs steady and well stretched downwards.
- The upper part of the body, easy, free and erect, with the hands low and close together without, however, touching each other or the horse and with the thumb at the highest point; the elbows and arms close to the body, enabling the rider to follow the movements of the horse smoothly and freely and to apply his aids imperceptibly.

This young rider has an excellent upright position. He has positioned himself for the turn ahead which will make it easy to stay in balance

The saddle in the picture above is straight but the rider's back is twisted making it difficult to keep the weight evenly distributed and to stay in balance with the horse

THE SEAT BONES

That is the goal and it is easiest to achieve if the rider has a broad base on which to balance, *ie* the seat bones wide apart and the buttocks relaxed. The two seat bones should rest evenly in the saddle and without moving out of it.

When trying to achieve a good position, the seat bones are the key points on which to focus and the rider has to learn both to distribute his weight equally on them and to ensure that he can keep them in the saddle at all times. This does not entail trying to sit heavily, as a rider's 'dead weight' makes it difficult for the horse to work 'through' his back. Such a rider often gets thrown out of the saddle because the horse stiffens his muscles and hollows his back against the dead weight. More effective is to stretch the back so it is as upright as possible without stiffening and then the hips can swing with the movement of the horse.

UPRIGHTNESS

It is difficult to achieve this crucial uprightness without tension, and some find it is easier to use images. The rider can think of balancing a water urn on the head like a peasant woman; or think of what it would be like to be a puppet with the main string holding the head and the rest of the body dangling below it. Either of these images results in a stretching of the spine with very little tensing of the muscles.

When the spine is stretched, the seat bones resting lightly and evenly in the saddle, and the muscles let go, the rider will have no problem in absorbing the movement of the horse. The horse will be able to work more easily with such a balanced weight and is therefore more likely to remain soft and supple in the back and to take elastic steps which are so much easier to sit than the tense, stiff steps that a heavy, rigid rider all too easily produces.

THE LEGS

From this stable positioning of his back it will be much easier for the rider to let his legs stretch downwards so they rest at all times on the horse's sides like wet rags. He will not have to hold himself in position by gripping with his thighs and knees.

THE SHOULDERS

Shoulders, too, are more likely to be free from tension and let go, so that the shoulder blades are flattened. Either rounding the shoulders or holding them back so that there is a hollow between the blades disturbs the balance and creates tension. When the shoulders are free from tension then the arms too can hang so the elbows are close to the sides, and the hands remain independent of any movement in the back (eg in rising trot). The ability to keep the hands still and independent of other body movement is an important aspect of good riding.

THE HEAD

The head is often neglected in the establishment of the position, but it is very heavy, and every change in its position affects the back and causes such reactions as a tipping of the spine to compensate for the change in weight distribution. It is crucial that the head stays upright above the body, that it is not tipped forward, back or to one side. Most good riders focus their eyes onto the poll of the horse but they do so by glancing downwards, not by allowing their head to fall forward. The head must never tip to one side as this leads to a collapse of the spine. Many riders look to the side and down on turns but they should keep the eyes on the same plane, and still focused on the poll.

This maintenance of the head directly above the body helps to avoid one of the most serious and common faults in the rider's position, the 'collapsed hip', when the rider brings one shoulder closer to the hip on the same side by bending his spine. This leads to uneven distribution of the weight on the seat bones which is unbalancing for the rider and the horse – both will have to tense their muscles.

Many riders find it difficult to divide their weight equally between the two seat bones, and this is a tricky problem to correct when actually riding the horse. If one tries to use corrections such as lifting the shoulder that is dropped, this usually entails trying hard, and results in tensing of the muscles and even more problems, albeit different ones.

It is of little value to achieve the correct position through rigidity and tension. The best way of straightening is to think positively, to work on the goal more than the corrections. Spend as much time as possible watching riders who sit in good straight positions, keep a picture of how they ride when riding oneself, keep thinking of straightening the spine and of lifting the head as if carrying a water urn, and try to work 'off' the horse.

If not straight when sitting in a chair or standing up, it will be very difficult to be so when on the horse. Most people with postural problems develop them through long hours of sitting at desks in collapsed, one-sided positions, or perhaps through shyness and nervousness which leads to uneven tension in groups of muscles. There are a variety of techniques for straightening the body, but one of the best known is the Alexander Technique, which helps to improve the poise, balance and coordination of a person. Unfortunately it cannot be learnt in a book, only in one-to-one lessons with an Alexander teacher. This technique has been used extensively by actors, musicians and dancers, and increasingly by dressage riders.

If not naturally supple the best place to develop this is off the horse. Aerobics, gymnastics, yoga are all ways of improving one's riding.

BALANCE IN MOVEMENT

It is relatively easy to stay upright, with the joints free and the muscles let go when the horse is standing still. It is a little more difficult to do this when the horse is walking in a straight line and even more difficult at the trot and canter.

At the trot the rider has to remain balanced while the horse takes springy steps. If he sits stiffly or heavily he will suppress the ability of the horse to work 'through' the back and will affect the elasticity of the steps. He will be responsible for the horse taking short, flat strides and losing much of his natural athleticism. He has to allow the horse to 'swing' through his back (see chapter 4). Therefore in sitting trot he must allow his loins, seat, thighs, knees and ankles to be free to absorb the movement but without losing his uprightness and balance. At the sitting trot, the feel is rather like riding the crests of small waves and is neither very smooth (when the strides would be very flat) nor very staccato, bouncing sharply up and down (when the strides would be short and stiff). The rider can avoid any tendency to bounce in the saddle and for the horse to stiffen against the weight, by rising to the trot. It is important that he should rise off both seat bones, that there is no twist to the movement, and that he changes diagonals when the direction changes, *ie* rises when the inside hind leg steps forward.

In a good athletic canter, the horse's back moves under the rider with the bounding-like strides of the pace. The rider must absorb this movement by stretching the spine upwards and allowing the loins, seat, thighs, knees and ankles to be free. The movement should not be absorbed – as it is very frequently – by moving the upper body back and forth as this is unbalancing, nor by sitting so stiffly and/or heavily that the spring of the strides is stifled and the moment of suspension suppressed.

TURNS AND LATERAL MOVEMENTS

Turning a corner or moving forwards and sideways in the lateral movements will also require adjustments in the rider's position. He will have to turn his body if he is to stay upright over the top of the horse *ie* if he is to keep with the horse he must turn as much as the horse does. Consequently the shoulders should turn to remain parallel with those of the horse. The head should turn, and as stated above it is very important that the eyes remain on the same plane, that the rider does not – as so many do – look inwards and down so the head tips on one side with the consequent loss of uprightness to the spine. The trunk also has to turn, but there are two different approaches as to what is done with the seat bones. At the Spanish Riding School the seat bones remain parallel with the shoulders, *ie* the whole of the back is turned in unison, with the outside seat bone coming forward. In the German school there is a twist to the turn with the inside seat bone coming forward so that together they follow the movement of the horse's hips, not the shoulders. Both are successful means of achieving the criterion of a good position, staying in balance with the horse.

For the rider to stay in balance, whatever the movements ridden, his shoulders must turn with those of the horse. The seat bones also move, either

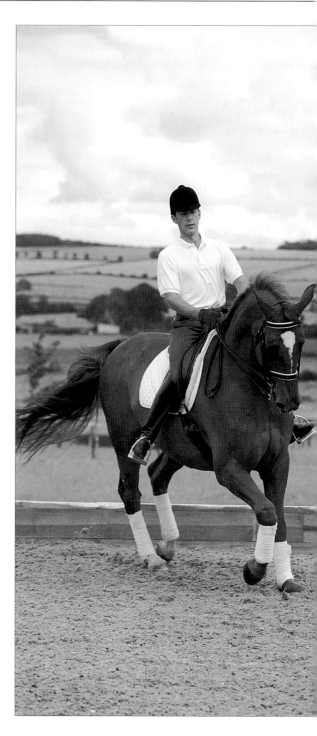

Horse and rider in a balanced turn. Ideally, the rider's inside leg should be further forward

to follow the rider's shoulders or the horse's hips. To achieve this the rider should not think so much of forcing a hip or a shoulder forward, but of staying upright and following the horse. If a rider has difficulty in doing this, then it is better to work from the premise of removing the tension which is stopping him from turning, rather than forcing a shoulder or a hip forward or back. Work on keeping upright, letting go and allowing the hips to swing rather than using strength to establish a position.

FEEL

Feel is what distinguishes a good dressage rider from an ordinary one. If the rider can listen to the messages the horse sends to him, not just give them himself, if he can feel when one hind steps forward more than another, when some of the muscles stiffen, when the flying change is late behind, or when on the wrong leg, then it will be much easier to correct problems.

Those with a very good sense of feel can tell what the horse is about to do, and therefore prevent an error before it happens.

The ability to feel is the natural talent of a horseman, but it can be developed with hard work. A rider feels when he holds his position without tension, so he can follow the horse's movements, and is not so rigid and stiff that he is independent of them. Therefore a good balanced position with free joints and muscles, is the basis from which feel can be developed. Then the rider must ask himself, and/or the trainer keep demanding, when the near hind is stepping forward, which diagonal he is rising on, which canter lead he is on, so that he becomes more alert as to what is happening beneath him.

COMMUNICATION: THE AIDS

The aids are the means of communication with the horse and in advanced dressage are applied with a high degree of precision which takes time and experience to learn. Different schools use different aids, and some theories are very sophisticated and complicated. Each rider has his own variations, and so the following is merely a practical and simple account, as the title of the book requires.

The key factors are that the aids are clear, used consistently in the same way and the horse is rewarded when he obeys by easing the aids and/or yielding the reins and/or patting or use of the voice.

The aids can only be applied imperceptibly, as required in the FEI rule book, if the rider has a good balanced position.

He has three lines of communication, the hands, seat and legs, and in dressage the hands are the least important. Their use, too, is preceded by and is less influential than the other two aids.

This pony has reacted well to the rider's aids to halt and is being given his reward – a pat

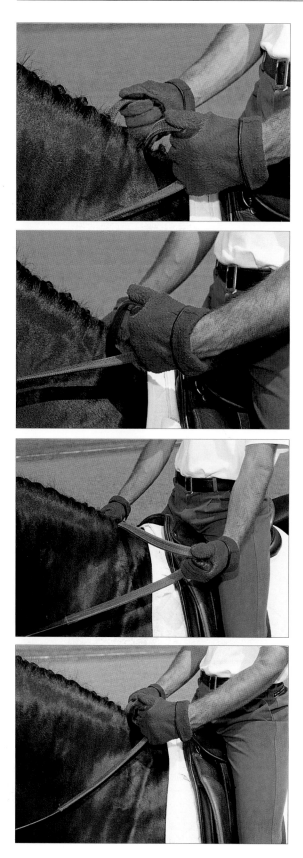

Four positions of the hands

a) normal

b) using the wrist

c) open rein

d) yielding

THE HANDS

It is instinctive to use the reins on their own as brakes, and they will slow down the horse, but at the expense of the hindquarters falling out behind and the weight going onto the forehand. Any increased pressure in the reins should come about because the legs – and more and more as training advances, the seat – direct the horse's fore into the reins more strongly. It is the legs which ask for contact with the hands.

The hands can be used in a number of ways. When passive they maintain a soft elastic contact which, especially with young horses, can be quite supportive, but never to the degree that the horse leans on the reins. When active the hand or hands can be used to yield the contact, to regulate it, soften it and to not allow. This can be done by varying the finger pressure and by slightly turning the wrist, but not by pulling back.

The reins when acting as brakes, to regulate the speed, are used in conjunction with the legs (and at later stages in training, the seat). The legs ask for the engagement of the hind legs so that the horse carries the weight more under his body, and this action is met with a stronger feel in the reins which is maintained so as to result in a downward transition, a shortening of the strides, a halt, or whatever is required, and is followed by a slight yielding of the rein.

The reins are used to turn a horse, but again only in conjunction with the leg and seat aids. The inside rein indicates the direction, but not by pulling back and only after the aids have been given from the inside leg, and the weight to the inside. The pressure of the inside rein is varied, and its position may be adjusted if the horse is not responding – with the young horse, bring it to the inside in an open rein effect, and with the trained horse towards the withers in the indirect rein position. The outside rein helps the balance in a supportive role, allows as much as is needed to achieve the required bend, and regulates the speed.

The reins are used, too, to contain the energy and momentum created by the rider's legs and seat, by the non-allowing action. The hands are kept in the same position so the rein pressure is not released and the horse is ridden up to them until he softens and relaxes his jaw when the contact is yielded slightly.

For much of the time the hands are simply receivers, being both the medium through which the rider can feel what is happening, and the soft elastic contact point to which the rider asks the horse to work towards with his leg and seat aids.

THE LEG AIDS

It is the leg and the weight aids which are the initiating aids, the ones that are applied first. For the young horse — before his back has strengthened and rounded — the leg aids are the most important.

As described above, the legs should rest on the horse's side like wet rags. They can be applied in a number of ways and with different effects. A leg aid when applied just behind the girth with quick, light variations in pressure, acts as a forward driving aid, a means of increasing impulsion. If it is used on one side only in this position, and in a quieter more supportive role, then it is an aid for a bend of the whole horse around it.

If the leg or legs are applied further behind the girth, then they will have a different effect. A leg aid that is active encourages the hind on that side to step forward and sideways. If left quietly on the horse's side, the leg will play a supportive role, stopping the hindquarters from swinging out to the side. If one is brushed back to behind the girth, it will indicate to the horse the leg on which he should strike off in the canter.

Top right: The leg applied behind the girth

Right: The leg applied by the girth

THE SEAT AIDS

The seat aids become increasingly important as the horse advances in his training. They are subtle aids and any rider that has not established a stable upright position and cannot keep his weight equally on both seat bones, is unwise to start trying to use them. The more skilled the rider, the more he can use his seat to control the horse. The weight can be transferred more onto one seat bone than the other. This is achieved by pressing down into the heel on the side that the weight is required, and not by shifting the seat sideways. The body must still remain upright and not lean in an attempt to get the weight onto one side. When the rider puts more weight onto one seat bone it helps the horse to move in that direction, in a turn, or in lateral movements half pass, travers, etc.

Much has been written on the use of the back in the application of the seat aids, and the manner in which this is achieved. There is considerable variety of opinion, and each rider tends to establish his own way of communicating with the horse. In general, if he leans back very slightly and tightens his buttock and back muscles momentarily so the position is

The seat being used with a collecting effect in half halt *(left)* and with a driving effect in extended trot *(right)*

fixed, this will increase the pressure on the two seat bones and encourage the hind legs to become more active and depending on the muscles used this can have two effects: if the muscles in the back are tightened and the back straightened upwards, this will have a restraining effect, as in transitions and collection; or if the tummy muscles are tightened and the back is very slightly rounded this will have the forward driving effect as used in extensions.

AUXILIARY AIDS

In dressage the auxiliary aids are the whip, spur, and voice.

THE DRESSAGE WHIP is a long one which can be used to reinforce the leg aids without the rider having to move his hand backwards. It is applied with a small turn of the wrist to give the horse a quick tap. It is important that this aid is applied so that it is understood by the horse as a reinforcement to the leg aid, and not as a punishment. The horse should react by becoming more active with his hindlegs either stepping more underneath or more sideways, and not by tensing up and jumping forward. If the horse does get anxious when the whip is used, it is important to spend time familiarising him with its

The long dressage whip being carried in a position from which it will be easy to use it to reinforce the leg aids

more gentle effects. When he is in the stable, tie him up and brush him along the sides with the whip. Before getting on him for a ride, run the whip over his body and tap is feet with it until he loses his fear.

SPURS are a means of adding more precision to the leg aids, especially with the more advanced horse. Their use is inadvisable on the young, untrained horse, unless he is exceptionally lazy when they can be used on one or two occasions to make him sharper and more alert. Spurs make possible more refined aids with the more advanced horse, but only if the rider has sufficient control over his legs that he uses them when intended.

THE VOICE is an effective aid especially in the training of the young horse before he has become fully receptive to the leg, seat and hand aids. If used in low tones it can have a soothing effect, short sharp tones will increase impulsion, and strong, gruff tones can be used as a reprimand. It should be remembered that the voice cannot be used in a test.

PHYSICAL FITNESS

If the rider is a passenger on the horse he need not be very fit, but he will not get very far in dressage. He has to be able to co-ordinate his aids, to drive the horse forward into the hands, to be constantly ready to readjust his aids and his weight to keep the horse balanced and going correctly, and he has to prepare the horse for the various movements. To do this well takes a considerable amount of fitness. For those with one, or even two horses to ride each day, it will be difficult to be fit enough to ride them well without doing extra fittening work.

Swimming is probably the best means of getting a dressage rider fit, as this exercises all the muscles and helps to promote suppleness. Bicycling, jogging, and sit-ups are other useful means of fittening. Jogging and bicycling help to build up the leg muscles, too, and sit-ups the stomach muscles.

Various loosening and stretching exercises also help to make the time in the saddle more worthwhile; for example: keeping the feet flat on the floor and the back straight, bend at the ankle, knee and hip joints to fold the legs so they are closer to the floor. With the arms pointed towards the ceiling, stand on tip-toes and spring from one foot to the other while stretching up as tall as possible. With the arms stretched out to the sides and parallel to the floor, swing around in the same way as when following the horse's shoulders on a turn.

If a rider finds it difficult to keep the heels down, this exercise may help: stand on the edge of a stair with the heels over the edge and allow them to stretch down towards the next stair.

Practise turning the head without allowing it to tip. Keep the eyes on the same plane. Check on this in front of a mirror. If the back tends to get rather hollow, stand against a wall and while keeping the back against the wall, slide towards the floor by bending at the knees. Allow the waist to fall back towards the wall so that the hollow disappears.

Magazines, the television and books are full of exercises that help to improve fitness and suppleness; most are beneficial, as long as they are not so difficult that they cause tension.

MENTAL APPROACH

The ability to switch into a state of relaxed concentration is important for a good dressage rider. Tension makes it difficult to stay in balance, to move with the horse and to co-ordinate the aids. A lack of concentration makes it difficult to prepare for and do the movements. This state of relaxed concentration is important to all sports and there are a host of books, tapes and so on, on mind–body techniques and the psychology of sport. It is beyond the scope of this book to study the subject in detail, but anyone ambitious to succeed in dressage should certainly do some courses or read up books on this subject.

Deep breathing is one of the simplest ways of becoming more relaxed when tension starts to grip, and it is something that can be done at that tension-provoking moment, just before going into the arena for the test.

HOW TO LEARN

The foregoing are the aims for the dressage rider, and the following are ways of working towards achieving them.

WATCHING

Dressage is an activity in which one of the most valuable aids to improvement is simply watching others who do it well. One of the reasons that Germany is so good at dressage is that groups of riders train together in clubs, giving them plenty of opportunities to work together and watch others of a high standard.

Every possible chance should be seized to go and watch training clinics, competitions, and to travel abroad to see the shows and training centres. Videos are a less time-consuming means of watching the top riders and there is now an extensive range of videos of training and major competitions. Watching these again and again will help in the establishment of a good position and clarification of what is a good walk, trot, canter, and a particular movement.

TRAINING

A good trainer will give a rider a system to work by and develop his ability. Working on one's own in dressage can lead to many pitfalls. It is easy to fall into bad habits and/or for the horse to push the rider into a poor position. With a person on the ground to point out problems the rider can correct them at an early stage.

Especially when learning the basics of dressage, regular lessons are very important. Videos taken of training sessions and tests are also helpful as then the student can see for himself what the trainer or assistant tells him is the problem.

LUNGEING

Being lunged is an excellent means of establishing a balanced position, of learning to feel, and how to use the aids. The rider does not have to worry about how the horse is going, and as long as the lunger is experienced and the horse works sufficiently correctly for the rider to sit to the trot with ease, he can concentrate on his own position. The horse must establish a good rhythm to the trot. It is best to lunge him without the rider at first to rid him of any freshness and tendency to buck. Side reins should be worn, tight enough to maintain a contact, but not so tight that the horse overbends.

On the lunge the rider can learn to keep his

This rider is being lunged so that she can focus on her position and establish a balanced seat

stable position, to balance evenly on both seat bones, and to let go the muscles so that the buttocks fall around the saddle rather than are held up off it. The legs and back should be stretched respectively down and up, and without creating tension in the muscles.

To achieve this, the rider can at first hold on to the saddle, but as he becomes more accustomed to this way of riding, can lift first one hand into the rein position, then both. Start at the walk, then trot, but only try at the canter when very stable and riding a balanced horse.

There are various exercises which help to make the rider more supple, poised and stable which can be performed in the saddle. He can bend his knees and lean forward to establish a position like a jockey at the trot, and then revert back to the dressage position. He can swing his legs alternately back and forward from the hips. He can take both legs off the saddle and then allow them to fall back down into the correct position (this is difficult to do at the trot, and novice riders should just take their legs off at the halt and walk). It is an exercise which can be

used with tremendous benefit when riding as it helps to free the hip joints, release tension in the legs and ensure that the rider is not gripping onto the saddle. Many top riders take both legs off the saddle momentarily, even in the middle of a test.

Another useful exercise on the lunge is to turn the ankles in circles to loosen up these important joints. The arms can be taken out to the side so that they extend horizontally from the shoulders and then the rider can turn them as far as possible clockwise and then as far as possible anti-clockwise. One arm at a time can be swung round in a circle; and the hands can be put on the points of the shoulders and the shoulders shrugged.

All of these exercises help the rider to loosen up, to stretch his limbs, and to make his joints free, but they are only of value if they can be done relatively easily. Therefore start them at the walk and only progress to the trot when a pretty stable position has been established.

This is vaulting at the highest level, pictured at the World Equestrian Games

The rider can also develop his ability to feel on the lunge. He can learn to feel which hindleg is moving forward, firstly at the walk and then at the trot. In the beginning the person who is doing the lungeing can say which leg is coming forward, but as the rider relaxes he should start to say what is happening himself. He can learn to feel when the horse's back muscles are stiff and hollowed against him, and when they are soft, elastic and the back comes up under the saddle, and there is a swinging motion which is easy to sit to. The rider can also learn to apply the aids. If the horse is sufficiently trained he can start a little shoulder in and travers on the lunge, as well as numerous transitions and half halts.

VAULTING
Vaulting is extremely popular with young people in Europe and is very good groundwork for a dressage rider. One horse is used for several students, which makes it a relatively cheap form of lesson. The horse is lunged, and has to be able to go around in a steady rhythmical canter. Students learn to vault onto the horse, stand up on him and do various exercises, which is fun and helps them to become balanced, to understand the motion of the horse, and to co-ordinate their own bodies.

RIDING WITHOUT STIRRUPS
Lunge work is done without stirrups, but it is also useful to cross your stirrups and ride without them during work sessions, or even when riding-in at shows. This helps to establish a more balanced seat that is not reliant on the stirrups, but it should only be done at the trot and canter when the horse has loosened up and is letting go. If he is still tense and stiff, it will be hard for the rider to sit to him and any bouncing in the saddle will only make him and the rider more tense and stiff. Therefore only cross the stirrups after the horse has been well loosened up and only if he goes in a manner which is easy to sit to, otherwise this exercise is counter-productive.

THE SCHOOLMASTER

One of the greatest aids to learning dressage is to ride a horse which knows what he should be doing – if the rider is having to teach the horse, it is very difficult to teach himself at the same time. The novice dressage rider should seize any chance to ride a schoolmaster, as the more experienced horse can give the rider a feel of the movements and way of going so he can find out what he should be aiming towards when he trains a novice horse.

TRYING TOO HARD

One of the biggest handicaps to improving dressage riding is trying too hard. As soon as a rider tries to do something too assiduously, he stiffens, making it more difficult to do so. He must make a great effort to do the work that will help him to improve, but he must remain relaxed enough so that the body can do what is required.

There are various aids to achieving this. Many riders use yoga, the Alexander Technique and even meditation. If they are to control their horses they must have control over their own bodies. For some people this is natural, but many, especially those who take up dressage at an older age, will benefit from the assistance of such techniques off the horse. Some riders find it easier to learn and improve through imagining what they want to achieve, rather than thinking of how to achieve it; for example, if told to keep the heels down, the hands steady, the head still, trying to put these orders into effect often leads to that inhibiting tension. If they imagine riding like Nicole Uphoff or Carl Hester they may achieve better results.

Although the end product is the same – a balanced, upright seat – different learning processes can be used to suit the rider. Some develop quickest in the old-fashioned way of being subjected to direct orders, others benefit from the growing number of techniques and approaches that avoid the use of the intellectual, logical, critical left brain and develop the intuitive, artistic right brain. If you find it difficult, for example, to keep your heels down when the instructor tells you to do so perhaps you are trying too hard, and a more effective means might be by use of images and the Inner Game techniques. It is easy to do dressage, but hard to do it well; if you are finding it difficult to acquire that good position through traditional teaching, then explore other approaches.

3

The Test

The aim of today's dressage riders is to compete, to take up the challenge of performing a set series of movements (the test) in front of judges who assess the quality of training and how well the work is done on each occasion.

This twentieth-century approach to dressage is based on, but is pretty different from, that of the past. The first who were known to practise dressage were the Greeks in classical times whose mastery of this challenging art was proven by depictions on the Parthenon frieze. Its popularity died out with their empire, however, and was not revived until Renaissance times in Italy. The courts of Europe then took it up with eagerness, the young noblemen practising it to prove their skills and superiority, and the ladies and older members finding the displays of horsemanship, usually to music and with riders in extravagant and colourful dress, pleasing entertainment.

An Iberian horse, the type that has long been used for Classical dressage

For three hundred years such theatrical dressage was a feature at all the continental courts, but with the destruction or decline of so many of the empires and regimes, the cavalry became the major exponent of dressage. Dressage became more practical, good exercises for the troopers, and when it was introduced into the Olympic Games at Stockholm in 1912 it was more of an obedience test, with horses having to show their willingness to go past strange objects.

The goal of Olympic participation meant that standards and interest rose rapidly, greater demands were made on contestants and increasingly, gymnastic ability was tested alongside discipline. By the 1936 Olympic Games at Berlin all the movements now used in top international tests had been added, piaffe and passage being introduced that year.

The cavalry remained the strongest force in competitive dressage until the 1960s, so the training required to do well in tests was an extension of that required for a good troop horse. This meant the demands of the tests were rather different from the dressage practised in the courts in past centuries. There was more emphasis on forward movement and extension, less on collection, more on discipline and accuracy, less on fluency and aesthetic effect, more on suppleness and elasticity, less on lightness and elegance.

The more traditional form of dressage was still practised, and to music, by its custodians the Spanish Riding School and various schools in the Iberian Peninsula including the late great master Nuño Oliveira. Competitions and old schools used to be representative of diverging approaches, but now, with more and more competitions, including music freestyles as well as the more technical straight tests, and a tendency towards favouring lighter horses and more stylish riding, competitive dressage is swinging back towards older standards and the divergence is merging.

Schools in the Iberian peninsula practise the more traditional forms of dressage that include 'airs above the ground'

THE ARENA

Competitive dressage is performed in an arena which is 20 metres wide. For all international and many national tests it is 60 metres long, but a shorter arena can be used which is just 40 metres long. At specific points around the arena are letters to indicate the places where movements should begin or end. There is no known documentation as to when the letters were introduced or why they should be positioned in such an irrational order.

INTERNATIONAL AUTHORITY

The ruling body of international competitive dressage is the Fédération Équestre International which is based in Bern. They are responsible for the tests and judging of the four senior levels of international dressage – Prix St Georges (the easiest), Intermédiaire I, Intermédiaire II and Grand Prix. There are also special tests for pony riders, juniors and young riders on horses. The FEI oversee the international shows and the annual championships – European/Pan American every two years alternated with World Equestrian Games and Olympic Games which each occur every four years.

The Grand Prix is the test which decides the team event at these championships, and includes all the classical dressage movements other than those asking for extreme extension of the forelegs (Spanish walk) or the 'airs above the ground' (levade, capriole, etc). The top riders in the Grand Prix go forward to the Grand Prix Spécial which has the same movements as the Grand Prix but they are asked for in more difficult places and ways. The top riders from this go forward to the Music Freestyle (Kür) and the percentages from the three tests added together to determine the individual medal winners.

The newest field for international dressage is the music freestyle in which competitors perform certain specified movements but in any order and to music of their choice. It is used at all levels of dressage. There is too a championship in which the focus is on the Freestyle; qualifiers for it are staged throughout the world. It is known as the World Cup and is at Grand Prix level.

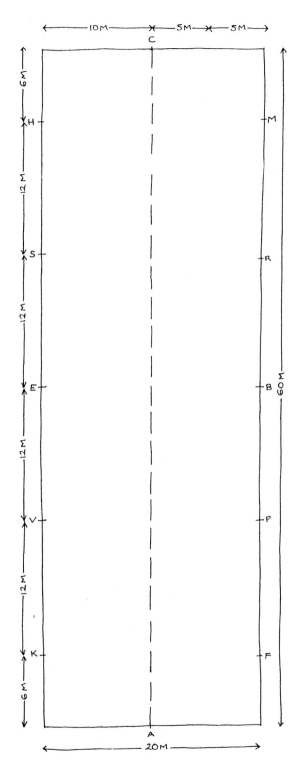

For all international and many national tests the arena is 20 metres wide by 60 metres long. In the 20 x 40 metre arena there are no markers for P, R, S and V

NATIONAL ORGANISATION

Countries all over the world are finding that interest in dressage is growing rapidly, and in many it is the fastest growing equestrian sport. National federations follow the FEI formulas, using FEI tests at the higher levels, their approach to judging and their directives as to how movements should be performed.

At national levels there are tests for juniors (usually within the Pony Club) and a series of progressively more difficult levels. In Britain, tests run from preliminary, through novice, elementary, medium, advanced medium, and advanced before reaching FEI levels. In the USA, national stages are training, 1st, 2nd, 3rd and 4th, again culminating in FEI tests. Most countries have a system of grading so that after winning a specified amount the horse is upgraded to the next level.

TESTS

The aim is to test the training of the horse which makes dressage a little different from other equestrian sports. Competing in itself does not help to advance the horse's training and make him any more ready for the next stage, as in show jumping. The horse is advanced at home during training, and the competitions are only there to test that the training is correct, and that the horse is progressing according to classical principles. Most experienced riders like their horses to be working at a higher level at home than that at which they are competing. If a horse is asked to do a movement he is only just learning at a particular marker in the arena he will often find it difficult, and may start resisting and stiffening, all of which will set back the training.

In competition-orientated countries like Britain and America, tremendous value is placed on participating in events and winning rosettes, but dressage has added value in that the training at home is also challenging and satisfying and many riders train their horses to Grand Prix levels without ever trying to compete. The long-term progress of a horse is soon set back if he is made to do numerous competitive tests of his training, especially if he has barely reached that standard.

A tests consists of a series of movements, about a dozen at the easiest levels but thirty or more at the highest. When a horse completes a movement, the judge notes the faults and good points and then summarises with a remark and awards an appropriate score out of 10. For excellent the mark is 10, very good is 9, good 8, fairly good 7, satisfactory 6, sufficient 5, fairly bad 3, bad 2, very bad 1, and not executed is 0.

At the more advanced levels some of the movements are given coefficients, usually x2, for example for the extended walk, so this then has added significance. Also the way in which the scores are distributed often gives much greater weight to a particular sector of a test than onlookers realise. Transitions between paces may be given a single mark of their own, so that a slight stiffening when a horse goes from walk to canter can lose just as many marks as when a horse commits the much more obvious fault of, say, breaking into a canter in an extended trot. This is why competitors must study the distribution of marks carefully to see where they must concentrate hardest on getting it right. It also explains why spectators who judge their winners by easily-seen mistakes and general way of going often do not understand why another competitor received such a particularly high total.

At the end of the test sheet are the collective marks which assess the horse and rider for their way of going. These are discussed in more detail in chapter 4, but in FEI and in an increasing number of national tests these are categorised as: the paces – the natural ability of the horse, and how well the rider has balanced him to retain the regularity and freedom of the paces. The impulsion – the power of the horse to be able to go forward fluently and elastically, to lengthen his strides or to shorten and heighten them. The submission – the control over the horse, that he submits willingly and happily, is light in his movement, that the power is containable and he does not stiffen and resist. The rider – that he sits correctly, in balance, gives imperceptible aids and produces good results.

FREESTYLES

The new and fast-expanding form of competitive dressage is the music freestyle. This is a more artis-

tic form of dressage and as such is more liable to subjective (as opposed to objective) judging, but the pleasure brought to spectators is turning dressage into a sport which can provide good entertainment. Competitors have to accept the vagaries of a system of judging which has less clearly defined guidelines, in the interests of making their sport more aesthetic and fun.

The freestyle test sheet is divided into two sectors, the technical and the artistic. The technical is for the movements specified in the test, just like a

Anky van Grunsven and Bonfire who have won many championships in the Music Freestyle (Kür)

straight test but done in any order; and the artistic is divided into rhythm, energy and elasticity; harmony between horse and rider; choreography, use of arena, inventiveness; degree of difficulty, well calculated risks, and choice of music and interpretation of music. National tests have variations on this international way of judging the artistic sector of the Music Freestyle.

JUDGES

These are very important people as they set the standards which competitors will then try to achieve. If they point out a fault, most competitors will accept the criticism and train towards correcting it. This gives the judges a great deal of power as to the direction dressage takes and the training on which riders concentrate. This is in addition to the power they have to make some unhappy, others contented by determining the order of each class.

The official training of judges is based on classi-cal principles, and particularly the directives laid down in the FEI rule book. This official training starts initially at national level with seminars and tests whereby candidates can upgrade and qualify to judge progressively higher standards of tests; it is then taken over by the FEI when the judge is given the rank of international candidate judge by his or her national federation. After attending international seminars and judging at international shows, the most competent will become fully qualified international judges and ultimately official international judges.

To become a good judge, however, means acquiring much more technical experience and knowledge than there is time for on official courses. It is difficult to be a good judge without having ridden at advanced standards, and it is certainly neces-

At major events the judges sit in boxes, but at most normal shows the car is a good base from which to assess competitors. This judge is positioned at E on the long side of the arena

sary to read extensively, to study and watch whenever possible the best instructors and competitors training and competing, and to discuss endlessly with the various authorities, the reactions to, and assessments of, training and tests.

A judge must have great powers of concentration – one glance away, one blink of the eye and he might have missed a mistake such as an uncalled-for change of leg. He has to have a very clear idea of the standards which he is going to apply to all the competitors, and ensure that he does not become more or less lenient after hours of watching those competitors doing the same movements again and again. He must also be able to summarise and assess just how much a particular fault should be marked down within that movement. He must be able to see the whole picture and not become obsessed with particular faults like overbending or lack of engagement.

It is a difficult task, and one without the rewards of rosettes and trophies but usually only criticism from poorly marked competitors and the press who are keen to create as much excitement as possible. Each mark has to be given very quickly at the end of each movement. The judge will try and justify a poor one, certainly if it is 5 or under, with comments about the faults. If there is time he usually tries to point out the good factors. All comments are taken down by a writer onto each competitor's test sheet which will be handed to him at the end of the class.

Test sheets are collected, and scorers then add the marks up and the totals are made public. Most major events use computer systems enabling scores to be announced as the competitor leaves the arena. Some events do use electronic scoring so that as the judge says his mark, another assistant presses the appropriate button which lights up the figure on a board above the judges' box. This gives the spectators a much more interesting time, as they can learn about what is going on and see if they themselves can assess the standard of a movement before the judge gives his mark.

In international tests there are five judges, three of whom are positioned on the short side and one at the middle of each long side. In national tests there may only be one judge who is then always positioned on the centre line. The more judges there are, the more likely it is that any idiosyncrasies or mistakes can be averaged out. Judges are not infallible but they are, with surprisingly few exceptions, extremely fair, knowledgeable and honourable people, and this is fortunate, for dressage in its competitive form revolves around them.

SAMPLE MEDIUM STANDARD TEST

Arena: 20m x 40m   *Approximate time 5 minutes*

			Max. Marks
1.	A	Enter at collected trot	
	X	Halt. Immobility. Salute. Proceed at collected trot	
	C	Track right	
	CB	Collected trot	10
2.	BX	Half circle right 10 metres diameter	
	XE	Half circle left 10 metres diameter	
	EA	Collected trot	10
3.	A	Down centre line	
	DG	Shoulder-in left	
	C	Track left	10
4.	HXF	Change rein at medium trot	
	FA	Collected trot	10
5.	A	Down centre line	
	DG	Shoulder-in right	
	C	Track right	10
6.	MD	Half-pass right	
	A	Track right	10
7.	KXM	Change rein at extended trot	
	MH	Collected trot	10
8.	HD	Half-pass left	
	D	Collected walk	10
9.	A	Track left	
	FXH	Change rein at extended walk	
	HC	Collected walk	10 x 2
10.	DAF & HC	The collected walk	10
11.	C	Halt. Immobility. Rein back 4 steps	
		Proceed at collected canter right	
	CB	Collected canter	10
12.	B	Turn right	
	X	Circle left 20 metres diameter in counter canter	
	XE	Collected canter	
	E	Track right	10

			Max. Marks
13.	EM	Collected canter	
	MXK	Change rein at medium canter	
	Just before		
	K	Collected canter	10
14.	K	Collected trot	
	A	Collected canter left	
	AB	Collected canter	10
15.	B	Turn left	
	X	Circle right 20 metres diameter in counter canter	
	XE	Collected canter	
	E	Track left	10
16.	EF	Collected canter	
	FXH	Change rein at extended canter	
	Just before		
	H	Collected canter	10
17.	H	Collected trot	
	MBF	Collected trot	10
18.	A	Down centre line	
	G	Halt. Immobility. Salute	
		Leave arena at walk on a long rein at A	10
19.		Paces (freedom and regularity)	10 x 2
20.		Impulsion (desire to move forward, elasticity of the steps, suppleness of the back and engagement of the hind quarters)	10 x 2
21.		Submission (attention and confidence, harmony, lightness and ease of the movements, acceptance of the bridle and lightness of the forehand)	10 x 2
22.		Riders position and seat; correctness and effect of the aids.	10 x 2
		Total	270

Courtesy: **British Dressage**

SAMPLE INTERMEDIATE FREESTYLE TEST

Time allowed: Performance to be finished between 4 minutes 30 seconds and 5 minutes

Event	Date	Judge and position	No. in progr.		Competitor	Nation	Horse	No.

Technical marks

Event	Technical marks	Marks	Points	Coeff.	Final Marks
1.	Collected walk (minimum 20 m)	10			
2.	Extended walk (minimum 20 m)	10		2	
3.	Collected trot including shoulder in right	10			
4.	Collected trot including shoulder in left	10			
5.	Collected trot including half-pass right	10			
6.	Collected trot including half-pass left	10			
7.	Extended trot	10			
8.	Collected canter	10			
9.	Collected canter including half-pass right	10			
10.	Collected canter including half-pass left	10			
11.	Extended canter	10			
12.	Flying changes every third stride (minimum 5 strides consecutively)	10			
13.	Flying changes every second stride (minimum 5 strides consecutively)	10			
14.	Single pirouette in canter right	10		2	
15.	Single pirouette in canter left	10		2	
	Total for technical executions	180			

Movements of a higher level are not allowed.
However, travers, renvers, half-pirouettes are allowed.

Remarks

Signature of Judge

Artistic marks

Artistic marks	Marks	Points	Coeff.	Final Marks
16. Rhythm, energy and elasticity	10		2	
17. Harmony between rider and horse	10		2	
18. Choreography. Use of arena. Inventiveness	10		4	
19. Degree of difficulty. Well calculated risks.	10		4	
20. Choice of music and interpretation of the music	10		6	
Total for artistic presentation	180			

To be deducted

Time penalty:
more than 5' or less than 4'30'': deduct 2 points from the total of artistic presentation

Score (see conversion table)

	Points
Total for technical execution divided by 18	10
Total for artistic presentation divided by 18	10
Final score	20

In case two competitors have the same final score, the one with the higher marks for artistic impression is leading.

Courtesy: **FEI**

4

The Basics

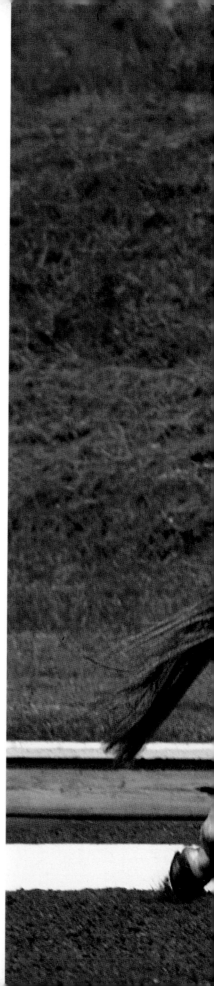

The ambition of most people who take up dressage is to find out how to do the 'tricks' – to go sideways, change from one leg to another, twirl around in pirouettes; however, if riders concentrate on these tricks, horses tend to stiffen up and lose forwardness. Good dressage riding is aimed at restoring the natural grace and beauty of a young horse when free, developing the horse's strength and co-operation so this natural talent is not spoilt but becomes more readily available. To do this the trainer must work on the basics – before the tricks, he must establish a good way of going for the horse.

When the basics are established, then not only will the horse's natural talents be more easily realisable, but it will also be much easier to teach the horse the movements. Many riders in their haste to earn competitive results – anxious to be able to say that their horse can do flying changes, or go sideways – forsake the foundations, the basics of dressage. They will pay the penalty, however, when competing against riders who pay attention to them, and will usually find it difficult to teach all the Grand Prix movements. The extra time spent on establishing the basics in a young horse will not only yield better competitive results, but in the long run will make it easier to do the tricks.

The judges take into account the basics in their assessment of each movement, but at the end of the sheet, three scores, usually with a coefficient of 2, are devoted entirely to the horse's way of going. These are known as the collective marks.

THE COLLECTIVE MARKS

The trainer must aim for his horse to move with those same free and balanced, springy (trot and canter), rhythmical paces that he did when free in the field as a youngster. Horses with good natural paces are light on their feet, appear to dance across the grass with an air or brilliance – this is what the trainer wants to retain and develop when the horse is ridden. He must take care not to distort the natural purity of the gaits (see below). It is the horse's paces, his natural talent, and how well his rider has retained and developed that talent, that the judges are looking for in the first of the collective marks in the tests – paces, their freedom and regularity.

The rider also wants power. Man's long association with the horse is based on admiration of his beauty and movement and the power the horse gives him to go faster and perform feats that would be impossible as a human. In dressage tests a major objective is to develop power, contain it and use it to make the work easier, more fluent and elastic. Movements could be done with the rider kicking away, but it looks and feels so much better if the rider can sit there containing the power so the horse moves easily into an extension or into step-

A horse free in the field, showing the stretching and rounding which is such a key part of establishing the basics

ping sideways. This is the second collective mark of the tests, impulsion: defined as the desire to move forward, the suppleness of the back, the elasticity of steps and the engagement of the hindquarters.

If the rider creates too much power, the horse becomes uncontrollable, hard to handle; if too little, he finds it difficult to do the work; in either case he resists, stiffens and objects. He may well do so for many other reasons – pain, lack of understanding, insufficient muscular development for the work, a bad rider; but whatever the cause the picture is spoilt. Nor is the 'feel' for the rider so good if harmony is lost, if the horse physically and/or mentally is not submissive – and this aspect of the way of going is covered by the third collective mark, submission: defined as attention and confidence, harmony, lightness and ease of the movements, acceptance of the bridle and lightness of the forehand.

These then are the aims of the rider in the arena: to have his horse going in such a way that his natural talents – the paces – are enhanced and not spoilt; that he has power; and that this is controllable so he is working in harmony. These three collective marks are the judges' means of assessing the horse's way of going.

THE SCALES OF TRAINING

In the training of the dressage horse, however, the way of going can be further divided and made more specific to provide more systematic foundations to the work. Various great French equestrian authorities have laid down the basics – General L'Hotte was the simplest with *Calm, Forward, Straight* – but it is the Germans who have the clearest, and most universally accepted definitions of the foundations. This is perhaps a reason for their awesome record of producing by far the largest number of top competition horses and riders. Every rider in Germany is brought up on 'the scales of training', and these are just as crucial for riding dressage as the scales are for playing the piano. These scales – rhythm, suppleness, connection, impulsion, straightness and collection – are, as national German trainer Harry Boldt so aptly describes, 'the golden

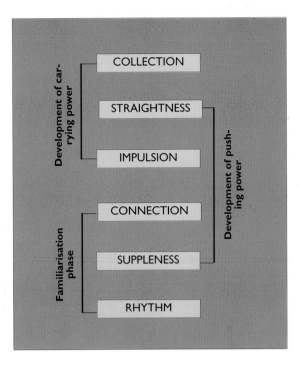

thread' from novice to Grand Prix levels.

The English translations are somewhat inadequate, for each of these scales means so much more in German than is immediately apparent from the word in English. *Takt* means much more than rhythm, *losgelassen* than suppleness, *anlehnen* than connection, and *schwung* than impulsion. Straightness and collection are the only satisfactory translations, so it is important to build up a fuller picture of rhythm, suppleness, connection, and impulsion than the usual English understanding of the word.

RHYTHM

Rhythm as the translation of *takt* has two aspects. Firstly the same rhythm is maintained, is pronounced, and like a metronome so there is no speeding up or slowing down. The tempo (speed of the rhythm) should not change. Secondly, the rhythm must be correct for that pace – the walk in a marching four-time, the trot two-time, and the canter three-time. This is the rhythm of 'pure' paces and must be maintained. The sequence must be correct and regular. Many horses lose regularity, usually through a loss of balance, sometimes when the steps are not even. An extreme irregularity is when the horse is lame.

BALANCE The key to ensuring the horse's rhythm is pronouced and correct is balance. A balanced horse will move as he did when free in the field with a pronounced and correct rhythm. The difficulty is that he has to learn to adjust to carrying a heavy weight on his back, and this is particularly unbalancing when he is first broken in, when he lacks the experience and strength as to how to cope with it. It will always be unbalancing if the rider does not himself have an upright balanced seat and/or does not know how to train the horse to carry this weight in a more balanced fashion *ie* by transferring the weight backwards off the forehand through engagement of the hindquarters.

This is a central aim in dressage: transferring the weight backwards so it is more evenly distributed and therefore easier for the horse to carry. When a horse is first ridden, he carries most of the weight on his forehand, making it difficult to maintain a rhythm to the paces, and leading to frequent changes of tempo. With good training he is taught to take progressively more and more weight off the forehand through gradually increasing the engagement of the hind-quarters. It takes time, for the muscles which will help him to engage need to be developed; there must be no tightening or resistance to this systematic transfer of the weight further back. When he learns to engage a little, he will be able to maintain the rhythm in straight lines and round corners, but as he engages more and more, the balance will improve so much that he will be able to maintain rhythm in half pass and shoulder in, and ultimately for the talented horse and rider, piaffe

and passage. Whatever the stage of the training, the principle of rhythm holds: it must be a constant tempo and correct sequence for each particular pace.

THE WALK The correct sequence to the walk is when the movement of a foreleg is followed by its diagonal hind, so the right fore goes forward before the left hind, then the left fore and finally the right hind. It is a marching pace so there is an equal interval between each leg's movement, a clear four-time rhythm. Some horses lose this sequence with the legs starting to move in lateral pairs, and sometimes not quite together so that the walk remains four-time, but with unequal intervals. If it deteriorates so both move together it is known as a 'pace', a two-time walk, and this is a serious fault. Riders can feel the lateral swing, and onlookers can see the lateral pairs moving together. A true walk is recognisable, as each lateral pair of legs will form a 'V' during a stride whereas in a 'pace' the legs will be parallel.

Unlike the trot and canter, there is no moment of suspension to the walk; there is always one or more leg on the ground.

THE TROT In the trot, the legs move in diagonal pairs with one diagonal pair leaving the ground just before the other returns to it to give a moment of suspension between each step. The legs of the diagonals should remain parallel and not, as can sometimes be seen in the medium and extended trot, the front legs taking more exaggerated steps than the hinds. It is also important that both hinds take even

The free horse is naturally balanced but has to learn how to maintain that balance under the weight of the rider. At first the weight is thrown onto the forehand but as training progresses the increasing engagement of his hindquarters help him achieve a better and better balance

The walk *The correct sequence to the walk is when the movement of a foreleg is followed by its diagonal hind, so the right fore goes forward followed by the left hind, then the left fore and finally the right hind. It is a marching pace so there is an equal interval between each leg's movement, a clear four-time rhythm. Some horses lose their sequence with the legs starting to move in lateral pairs, and sometimes not quite together so that the walk remains four-time, but with unequal intervals. If it deteriorates so both move together, it is known as a 'pace', a two-time walk, and this is a serious fault. Riders can feel the lateral swing, and onlookers can see the lateral pairs moving together. A true walk is recognisable, as each lateral pair of legs will form a 'V' during a stride whereas in a 'pace' the legs will be parallel. Unlike the trot and canter, there is no moment of suspension to the walk; there is always one or more leg on the ground.*

The trot *In the trot, the legs move in diagonal pairs with one diagonal pair leaving the ground just before the other returns to it to give a moment of suspension between each step. The legs of the diagonals should remain parallel and not, as can be sometimes seen in the medium and extended trot, the front legs taking more exaggerated steps than the hinds. It is also important that both hinds take even strides.*

The canter *The canter has a clear moment of suspension like the trot, but the beat is three-time. Unlike the walk and trot it is an asymmetrical gait with one lateral pair of legs – known as the leading leg – reaching further forward than the others. In the 'right' canter it is the right fore and hind, in the 'left' canter the left pair.*

The outside hind is the first to land after that moment of suspension, followed by the inside hind and outside fore and finally the leading leg, the inside fore. Horses that are slowed down too much without real collection often go into a four-time canter, when the inner hind does not land with the outside fore.

strides. Horses can take uneven steps in reaction to uneven rein pressure, uneven weight distribution in the saddle, or a physical problem. The trot is then said to be irregular.

THE CANTER The canter has a clear moment of suspension like the trot, but the beat is three-time. Unlike the walk and trot it is an asymmetrical gait with one lateral pair of legs – known as the leading leg – reaching further forward than the others. In the 'right' canter it is the right fore and hind, in the 'left' canter the left pair.

The outside hind is the first to land after that moment of suspension, followed by the inside hind and outside fore and finally the leading leg, the inside fore. Horses that are slowed down too much without real collection often go into a four-time canter, when the inner hind does not land with the outside fore.

Another fault is the disunited canter when the horse leads with the inside fore and the outside (not inside) hind. It usually occurs when a horse does a flying change, but only changes lead in front, not behind and is a very uncomfortable canter for the rider. Some horses with weak hindquarters or a physical problem may change the lead behind but not in front.

SUPPLENESS

The second of the 'scales' is 'suppleness' which is a limited translation of the German word *losgelassen*. It has been translated as letting go, loose, unconstrained and the important point is the absence of resistance. The muscles have tone, the joints are free and the horse's entire body can work without resistance.

A horse is supple when the back swings, shown by the tail being carried and oscillating rhythmically from side to side, and the rider being able to sit softly in the saddle, not thrown into the air by the horse's stiff back. The test that a horse is supple is for the rider to open the fingers so that the reins can slip through them – the horse should champ at the bit (with a closed mouth) so the reins are eased, not dragged, out of the rider's hands. If he stretches forward and down, then he has been letting go

A good indication of suppleness is when the horse is allowed to 'champ' the reins out of the rider's hands he stretches forward and down

those crucial muscles of the neck and back, he has been working with that important elastic muscle tone, and without stiffness.

The horse must be supple before any real hard work begins. At the start of each work session and at whatever stage of training, any horse is likely to have mental and/or physical difficulties in relaxing. He will be stiff after a long time in the stable, anxious about the surroundings and needs to be suppled up/calmed down until he lets go. It is likely, too, that during some work sessions he will be distracted, anxious about new lessons or even obstinate and stiff. He will resist and the state of suppleness must be restored as quickly as possible.

CONNECTION

The third of the 'scales' is connection. Often referred to as 'contact', I am happier with connection as this helps to emphasise the importance of the seat and legs in achieving it. The contact is a light, even elastic, feel in both reins, but the important fact is that this is achieved by aids from the legs (and seat) and not the hands.

Forward driving leg aids are applied to encourage the hindlegs to step more actively forward and the impulsive forward thrust thus created goes through the muscles along the horse's top line, and a connection is established between the hindquarters and the forehand. The rider feels the energy from the forward thrust coming through into the reins. The horse is connected with a round outline, and he is being ridden forward from behind into the rider's hands.

This is only possible if the horse is not running away, if he has established the first of the 'scales', rhythm. And it can only be done correctly if the second 'scale' is established, when the horse has let go the muscles of his back and neck, so the activity created in the hindquarters by the leg and seat aids can be transferred 'through' a swinging back, soft neck and poll into the hands.

The horse is worked from behind, not manipulated through the reins, so the crucial connection is developed between the quarters and the mouth. The rider should be able to feel in his seat and hands that this connection between the quarters and the mouth is derived from his seat and leg aids.

The horse should not lean on the hands, but maintain a soft elastic contact. The cause of becoming heavy in the hands may be over-eagerness when he will need calming down, but more frequently it is because he is falling onto his forehand. This is corrected by improving his balance, engaging the hindquarters through use of the half halt and transitions, not by trying to lighten the rein contact by use of the hands.

When he is first broken in, he will only be able to keep working 'through' his back, keep supple, if he carries his head and neck a little low, but as he becomes stronger, more able to engage and transfer the weight and balance backwards, so will he be able to lift his neck and lighten his shoulders, flex at the poll (which should be the highest point), and champ at the bit – and then he will be 'on the bit'.

Young horses are unlikely to take the contact evenly on both sides of the mouth. It is an objective that they should do so but it needs to be achieved gradually and through working the horse from behind, getting the hindlegs to take equal steps straight ahead, rather than by trying to fiddle with the mouth and rein contact. The hands should be

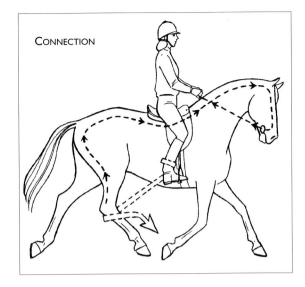

CONNECTION

kept steady receiving and controlling the energy generated from behind. Any pulling back affects the rhythm and the engagement of the hindquarters detrimentally.

IMPULSION

The fourth of the 'scales', impulsion, is much misunderstood. It is all too often confused with speed. As a collective mark in tests it is defined as the desire to move forward, but the French version is more correct – this is translated as the ability of the horse to carry himself forward *ie* that he has the physical power to do so, not just the mental will.

The source of this power is the hindquarters and the horse develops it by engaging his hindlegs, placing them further under his body so he is able to take springy rather than flat steps. This power will be reduced if the horse is not loose and supple, if he is not working 'through' his back, because the energy will be dissipated if the muscles are tense and resistant.

Impulsion is therefore contained energy created in the hindquarters. Containment is achieved by the rider's hands: the energy which has been transmitted through the back and neck is stopped from being used to make the horse go faster by the hands which restrain him with a soft, elastic contact. The strides then become elastic and springy in trot and canter. Impulsion is not seen when there is no moment of suspension to the pace, *ie* the walk.

Top: *Impulsion being used to produce a good extension to the strides*

Above: *Olympic Champion Gigolo showing a high degree of impulsion with those hinds well engaged, but this impulsion is so contained that he is barely moving forward, and is completing a canter pirouette*

When the horse can take these elastic, springy strides, he is able when asked by the rider to move forward with ease and to change fluently the length of his strides from short, collected ones into long, free, extended ones. His paces have more expression, brilliance and cadence. They are not spoilt by stiffness and tension, which flatten the strides.

The impulsion comes from the engagement of the hindquarters and the elasticity of his body. For a few horses this is natural and only needs nurturing, but for most horses it has to be developed by good training, by teaching the horse to engage his hindquarters and building up the strength that enables him to do this.

STRAIGHTNESS

The fifth 'scale' is straightness. A horse is straight on a straight line, when the hind feet step into the same tracks as the corresponding front feet, so that the horse is straight along his whole body. On a curved line the horse should be bent evenly throughout his body, enabling the hind feet to again step into the same tracks as their corresponding front feet.

Horses are born crooked and when we first start riding them, hardly ever adhere to the above definition of straightness. Even with good training, it is very rare to find a horse which is absolutely straight. Most horses tend to carry their right hind leg to the inside of the right foreleg, which transfers the weight diagonally across onto the left shoulder. This puts more weight onto it and the left rein, which makes the contact in the right feel much lighter. In a few cases, it is the other way, with the stronger contact being felt in the right rein.

One of the first things many riders try to do with young horses is to fiddle with the hands in an attempt to establish a more even rein contact. They tug strongly on the left rein (if that is the one with the firmer contact). There is then an inevitable tendency to pull back which will restrict the impulsion, contact, suppleness and rhythm. With the young horse it is best to concentrate on these earlier four 'scales', ensuring the horse is truly going forward with impulsion, and these will help to make him straighter. Later more focus can be put on straightness.

Most riders like to work on the straightness by

This pony is very straight with the hindlegs stepping directly towards the corresponding forelegs

From the hindquarters to the head this pony is straight

the stiff side by asking for a big bend in that direction, but with the reins only and this results in a bend in the neck but little, if any, in the body. All that happens is that the horse takes his neck in the direction asked through flexing it at the wither, and in so doing sends the weight onto his opposite shoulder. The aim, however, is to get the horse to bend evenly throughout his body with the rider's inside leg being the part around which he bends and not the wither. Therefore concentrate on shoulder fore (p97), shoulder in (p98) and circles (smaller circles to his stiff side and larger ones with very little bend to his hollow side), to straighten the horse.

COLLECTION

Collection is the last of the 'scales' and is the most difficult in so far as it needs the establishment of the other scales before it can be achieved correctly. Also the horse needs to develop muscular power if he is to be able to lower and engage his hindquarters, to shorten and heighten the steps for collection.

Collection is the central aim of many dressage riders. It is important to truly understand what it entails and the FEI put the objectives clearly:

1 To further develop and increase the balance and equilibrium of the horse, which has been more or less displaced by the additional weight of the rider.
2 To develop and increase the horse's ability to lower and engage his hindquarters for the benefit of the lightness and mobility of his forehand.
3 To add to the ease and carriage of the horse and make him more pleasurable to ride.

The shortening of the steps for collection is achieved by engaging the hind legs, necessitating the bending of the joints and the bringing forward of the hind legs under the horse's body. The rider asks for this with his leg and seat aids. The steps are not shortened by excessive use of the hand aids, as then, although they might well become smaller, they will also become flat and inactive; impulsion and engagement will be lacking and so too will rhythm, suppleness and connection.

Collection is marked by energetic use of the hind legs which step well under the body to result in the

using the shoulder fore and the shoulder in, exercises which are only started after rhythm, suppleness, connection and impulsion have been well established. When trying to straighten the horse, concentrate on the hindquarters and on getting the hind legs to step evenly and squarely under the body rather than varying rein pressure to get an even rein contact. When thinking about the rein contact it is best to tackle this the opposite way to what is natural, *ie* establish a firmer contact in the rein in which the horse is taking light contact, rather than starting a tug-of-war to get a lighter one in the rein in which he is strong.

Frequently riders try to supple up their horse on

forehand lightening and the neck and head coming out of the wither in a smooth curve with the head just in front of the vertical. A collected horse is light, manoeuvrable and has the impulse to be able to go forward into extended paces with ease.

The acquisition of collection is gradual, and there are varying degrees of it. A great deal of collection is needed for the most advanced movements in dressage, the piaffe and canter pirouettes, but a young horse cannot be expected to acquire such collection without adversely affecting the other basics. Therefore in medium and the easier advanced tests in which collection is required, its degree – ie the amount of engagement, lightening of the forehand and raising of the neck and head – is much less than that required in Grand Prix.

The development of collection is progressive and gradual. Trainers need to be constantly working towards more collection but whenever it is achieved at the expense of other basics, then less demands must be made on the horse and more elementary work returned to, to re-establish those other crucial scales of training.

Rhythm, suppleness, connection, impulsion, straightness, and ultimately collection, are the aims to retain throughout all the work. The young horse will not be able to achieve any of these scales at a very high level, and the trainer must be patient and realise the work is progressive. It is a mistake for a trainer to concentrate too much on any one of the scales, as each and every one of them helps the development of the others.

The basics have been established to a satisfactory level in a novice horse when he accepts a light elastic rein contact which can be ridden to with the seat and legs, and his hindlegs are linked/connected through a swinging, soft back, an unconstrained neck, and supple poll to the mouth. The horse is working 'through', and the rider is in control of the horse's natural athleticism.

5

One Track Movements

The following two chapters on movements are in text-book-like format for easy reference and the clearest possible understanding. They are organised into groups of similar movements and not in order of introduction during the training of the horse. This would be difficult as the timing varies according to the horse and rider, but the chart in chapter 7 does indicate the level of training when each movement is introduced.

The dressage movements asked for in the arena test the level and quality of the training, and in training are used to improve the quality of the work. In pursuance of each of these objectives those basic 'scales' of training must be maintained; there must be rhythm, suppleness, connection, impulsion, straightness and at the higher levels collection in all the work. They are representative of the quality of the way of going, and the essence of dressage is not that a movement was completed (ie that a shoulder in maintained an angle of 30 degrees to the track), but the way it was done (ie turned off the track and still kept the rhythm, the suppleness, the connection, impulsion, straightness and collection).

In the following discussion on movements, the basics should be mentioned each time as being part of the aim, and their loss as one of the common faults. This would, however, take up a great deal of space so it is assumed the reader has understood their importance by now.

The aids given in the following two chapters are only guides. There are many different ways of achieving good results, ie in a turn some riders keep their seat bones parallel with the horse's hips, others with the shoulders, in a shoulder in some put their weight to the outside, most keep it to the inside. The primary objectives for the rider are to make the necessary adjustments so that he is always upright and balanced in his position, and to focus on the aims, making adjustments to the aids as necessary to achieve the aim. Establishing a very clear picture of what to aim and feel for is much more important than learning the methods of how to do it as these will vary according to the many different circumstances. Remember too dressage riding is not push-button riding, but putting the horse in a position physically and mentally that he will find it easy to do the movements. The aids given below should be one means to achieving those aims, but if for example the horse is stiff to one side, not so quick to respond to one of the leg aids, the rider slightly crooked, then adjustments have to be made to put the horse in the position from which the movement flows easily.

The movements discussed in this chapter are all on one track, ie the horse is straight, the hind leg stepping along the same track as the corresponding foreleg whether on straight lines or a curve.

THE FIGURES

A TURN

THE AIMS

1 In all turns/changes of direction the horse should follow the line of the turn with his body so that the fore and hind legs step along that same line. **NB** The smallest turn asked for in a dressage test is of the arc of a 6 metre circle (volte), but the novice horse which lacks collection would be expected to make a much less sheer arc (about an 8 metre circle).

2 The contact in both reins should be light and consistent. He should not lean on either one or both reins to get support.

3 There should be no change in the tempo (speed of the rhythm).

THE AIDS

1 Prepare with one or more half halts (see p71).

2 Adjust seat to position for a turn (chapter 2), with the weight to the inside (press down on the inside stirrup).

3 Rider's shoulders turn to keep in line with those of the horse.

4 Inside rein indicates the direction.

5 Outside rein is supportive, controlling speed and amount of bend.

6 Inside leg active by the girth to encourage the bend through the body, activity of the inside hind and maintenance of impulsion.

7 Outside leg passive behind the girth but ready to be more active if the quarters start to fall out.

Top, r to l: This sequence shows a good turn by a young horse. With a more advanced horse it will be easier to keep a lighter inside rein (see illustration p30)

Bottom left: Use of the inside rein has resulted in some overbending

Centre: Wrong bend – the horse is bending to the outside

Right: Too much bend with the weight being thrown onto the outside shoulder

COMMON PROBLEMS AND POSSIBLE CORRECTIONS

1 Speeds up – more half halts. Balance needs to be worked on. Do not ask for too sharp a turn.

2 Weight falls onto outside shoulder with tendency to drift outwards. This problem is usually associated with too much bend in the neck with the central point of the bend at the wither rather than around the rider's inside leg – more positive action with outside rein, less with inside, shoulder fore positioning momentary flexion to the outside (counter flexion) which will help bring the shoulders back in front of the quarters. Ensure rider is staying in balance *ie* shoulders turned to remain parallel to those of the horse. Often caused by the rider being behind movement of turn, not turning his body-shoulders enough.

3 Quarters falling out – less inside rein, more support with outside leg and rein.

4 Leans on inside rein, not flexing and remaining light – more inside leg, more positive contact in outside rein, shoulder fore positioning.

5 Losing impulsion – increase use of inside leg. Probably too sharp a turn for stage of training, try less sheer curves.

6 Hindquarters falling in – ride forward more positively with both legs, but with outside leg closer to the girth than normal, think of shoulder fore positioning.

NB Many of the problems in turns are due to rider not staying in balance. If the rider does not stay upright, if his weight slips to the outside, if his shoulders do not follow those of the horse, then he is not in harmony with the movement and he will be disturbing the action of the horse. Study chapter 2.

VARIATIONS ON THE TURN

These are defined below, but the aids, common problems and possible corrections are all similar to those discussed above.

CORNER

In right-angled corners the horse should follow the track of one quarter of a circle. The diameter of the circle will vary according to the level of training of the horse and the pace in which he is going. Make it a shallow arc (10 metres) or more with novice horses and at medium paces and never use less than a 6 metre circle arc.

VOLTE

This is a 6 metre circle. If larger it is called a circle.

CIRCLE

The size of a circle is always stated in a test *ie* 10 metre, 20 metre.

AIM

1 Horse turns same amount each stride so there are no corners but a fluid curve. To help achieve this, 'think' of circle as diamond shape, and as you leave one point aim for the next. If making a 20 metre circle from B, the points of the diamond would be B; 10 metres from X towards A; E; and 10 metres from X towards C along the centre line.

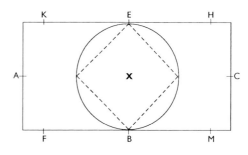

SERPENTINE
THE AIMS

1 This consists of a stated number of loops. Sometimes it is requested that the horse is straight as he crosses the centre line, sometimes that he makes the loops pear-shaped so that he comes across the centre line at the angle. As a training exercise the latter has a greater suppling

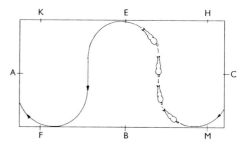

effect, making it easier to establish a distinct bend around the inside leg.

2 The first loop is started by moving away from the short side of the arena (*ie* do not go into the corner), and the last loop is finished by gradually moving in towards the middle of the opposite short side.

3 It is important to show a distinct change of flexion and bend as the horse crosses the centre line, while maintaining the same pronounced rhythm.

4 The loops should be of an equal size.

FIGURE OF EIGHT

This consists of two voltes or circles or equal size which are joined at the centre of the right.

THE AIM

I The horse should be straightened an instant before the change of direction at the centre of the figure of eight, and a clear change of flexion and bend shown.

THE TRANSITIONS

Transitions are made from one pace to another, within one pace from shorter to longer strides, or vice versa and from one movement to another.

THE AIMS

I To be at the prescribed marker, although for a novice horse the quality of the transition is more important than his accuracy.

2 To be smooth and fluent.

3 To retain the cadence (see Chapter 7) of the pace up to the moment of the transition and after it (unless coming to a halt).

4 Horse to remain connected, light in the hand and calm.

5 In transitions from longer strides to more collected ones the horse should take more weight onto the hindquarters, engaging them further under his body. He is ridden from behind into the hand and not vice versa.

6 In transitions within paces the tempo must be maintained so there should be no speeding up into extensions or slowing down into collection.

A transition from longer to shorter strides at the end of a diagonal. He is being ridden from behind into the contact

THE AIDS

These vary according to the type of transition.

I In downward transitions the aids are a series of half halts (see p71), *ie* momentary use of legs and seat to engage the quarters, and a momentary non-allowing hand to contain the effect and stop the horse from simply going faster.

2 In upward transitions: (a) for longer strides. The leg and seat driving aids are applied. When they increase impulsion sufficiently to be felt coming through the back to the hands, ease the hands so strides and outline can lengthen; (b) to a new pace, similarly leg and seat aids, but hands are only given sufficiently to allow into new pace, and not so much to allow the frame and the strides to lengthen.

3 Into canter, the aids are bilateral so as to establish the required leading leg. Establish a flexion to inside with inside leg and inside rein. Slightly more weight onto inside seat bone/inside stirrup. Control bend and speed (*ie* do not let run on in walk/trot) with outside rein. Outside leg brushed back behind girth to indicate required lead. Increased activity of inside leg aids, and lighten inside rein so horse can step forward.

COMMON PROBLEMS AND POSSIBLE CORRECTIONS

1 Abrupt – usually due to heavy use of rein aids and not enough leg and seat.

2 Hollowing, resisting, not remaining connected – try on a circle but usually due to horse not being 'on the aids', not coming 'through'; work on the basics. Transitions are one of the best ways of assessing whether the basics have been properly established.

3 Coming above bit in upward transitions – usually due to lack of preparation and impulsion; use more half halts.

4 Falling onto forehand in downward transitions rather than hindquarters engaging and forehand lightening – more half halts before transition, more engagement and ensure not pulling on reins *ie* ride from the hindquarters into the hand, not the front to the back, use the voice (but not in the test) so do not have to use such strong rein aids.

Top, l to r: The trot walk transition. In the second photograph the rider has applied the aids and the horse has engaged but tightened. This tightening is only momentary as a good walk is shown in the third picture

Bottom left: The rider has used softer aids to the walk and the horse has remained rounder than before (see centre top)
Centre: The rider has taken back the inside rein and the horse has overbent
Right: The horse lost his roundness, hollowed his back and lifted his head when the aids for the transition were applied

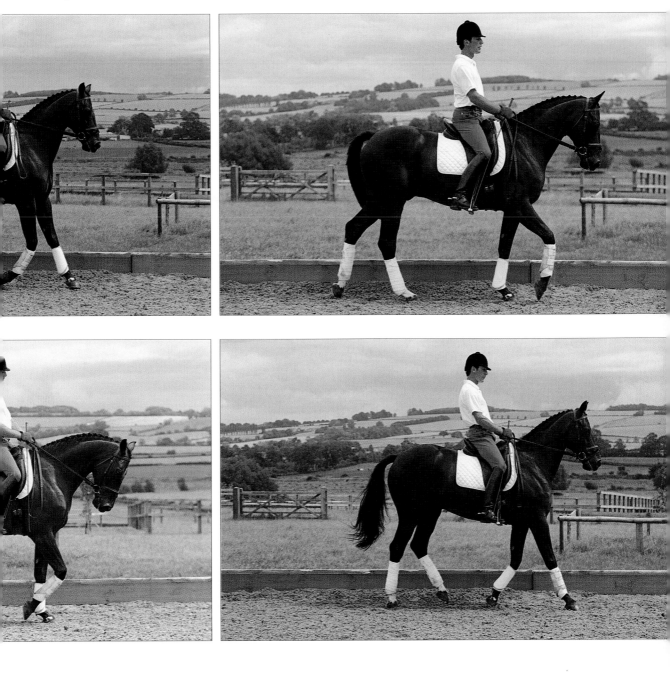

THE HALT

THE AIMS

1 To remain on the bit (he may champ at it) with the neck raised, the poll the highest point and the head slightly in front of the vertical. The contact should be light and soft.

2 The horse should remain attentive, motionless and ready to move off from the lightest aids.

3 He should be straight, with the weight evenly distributed on all four legs so that the front legs are parallel, and ideally the hinds too ie a square halt, but at very novice levels one hind may be slightly further behind.

4 For the horse to engage his hindquarters, and put more weight onto them.

THE AIDS

1 Leg aids used in a supportive manner to encourage the hindquarters to come further under the weight.

2 Seat aids used, but only lightly with a young horse, to achieve as in 1 above.

3 1 and 2 drive the horse towards the hands which restrain so there is no further movement.

4 Leg, seat and hand aids are applied momentarily, then relaxed, re-applied, and so on until the horse comes to a halt, then …

5 the seat aids are relaxed very slightly – it can help to keep the horse on the bit if the rider slightly displaces his weight backwards, and at the same time allows slightly with the hands (without loosing the contact), as this encourages the horse to relax and discourages him from stepping backwards.

COMMON PROBLEMS AND POSSIBLE CORRECTIONS

1 Abrupt halt – too much use of hand and/or jammed on rather than applied in a series of half halts.

2 Lack of engagement, excessive weight on the shoulder with forefeet pounding into the ground rather than touching it lightly – usually too much use of hand, rider leaning forward; reduce hand aids, increase leg and seat aids, and ensure sitting upright.

He should be straight, with the weight evenly distributed on all four legs

3 Hollowing and coming above the bit – increase leg aids, lighten seat aids, put more weight in stirrup irons, return to basics to establish acceptance of aids so works 'through'.

4 Front legs not parallel – check rein pressure is even and that rider's seat bones are parallel, improve horse's balance.

5 Not immobile – use the voice when training, try to keep the horse relaxed, check the rein aids are not too strong, keep the legs 'clinging' and supporting the horse without kicking, do not try to fiddle in halts to make him stand square.

6 Not straight, quarters to one side – support with clinging leg on side to which they swing, make sure rein aids on opposite side not too strong, keep in slight shoulder fore position (see p97) to side that they swing, check rider's weight not falling onto side to which they swing.

HALF HALT

THE AIMS

1 To increase the horse's attention before he is about to be asked for a movement.
2 To improve his balance and degree of collection with a slight shift of the weight onto his quarters, increase of engagement and lightening of the forehand.

THE AIDS

As in the halt, but the effect of the leg and seat aids are more important and stronger than the hand aids. The aids are given almost simultaneously and only held momentarily.

1 Seat aids – applied to encourage activity and hindquarters to come further under the body.
2 Leg aids – applied to encourage activity and hindquarters to come further under the body.
3 1 and 2 drive the horse towards the hands which do not allow for an instant to encourage engagement and collection, then yield. This yield is crucial. The half halt should help to horse to come lighter in the hand and into better self-carriage.

COMMON PROBLEMS AND POSSIBLE CORRECTIONS

1 Hindquarters are not engaged, neck shortens – too strong hand aids, only after the leg and seat aids have been applied should the hands restrain.
2 Hollowing and coming above the bit – seat aids may be too strong for the stage of training, use more leg, less seat. Horse may not be accepting

The first stages of half halt: the rider is containing the horse well with his seat, leg and hand aids

aids through his body *ie* is resisting and needs further training in the basics.

RELEASING THE CONTACT

GIVE AND RE-TAKE THE REINS

THE AIMS

1 The horse should retain the same rhythm, not quickening or slowing down.
2 The movement should show that the horse is not supported or held in place by the reins so when they are released he should neither lurch onto his forehand nor throw his head upwards.

A clear release of the contact, and the horse is keeping his balance

THE AIDS

1 Prepare with half halts.
2 Push the hands forward and back in one continuous movement so that the rein contact is released for a short moment.

COMMON PROBLEMS AND POSSIBLE CORRECTIONS

1 Loss of rhythm – work on getting horse more balanced; better preparation with half halts, more support with leg and seat aids.
2 Hollowing – shows lack of establishment of basics and being held into an outline; work on basics.
3 Falls onto forehand – as in 1 above.

CHAMP THE REINS OUT OF THE HANDS

THE AIMS

1 As the rider eases the rein contact the horse should stretch forward and down.
2 He should not snatch the reins or lurch forwards.
3 Rhythm should be maintained ie no loss of balance, no quickening or slowing down of the strides.
4 He should remain active behind, rounding his back and neck as he stretches them. He should not hollow or fall onto his forehand.

THE AIDS

1 Maintain supportive leg aids while easing fingers so reins can be champed out of the hands.

COMMON PROBLEMS AND POSSIBLE CORRECTIONS

1 Snatches the reins out of the hands or lurches forward – help him to keep balanced with supportive leg and seat aids, resist this tendency with both hands and when balance is restored, ease the reins again.
2 Quickening of strides – half halt and re-balance.

The rider has eased the contact and the horse is taking the rein forward and down

3 Slows down – use more leg.
4 Hollows or falls onto forehand – has not been working correctly, work on the basics.
5 Does not stretch – work on basics and in particular suppleness.

STROKE THE HORSE'S NECK

THE AIMS

1 With contact completely released, the horse retains same outline, rhythm, balance and engagement for a few strides.
2 To show that horse has self-carriage and sufficient collection (engagement of hindquarters) to continue in same way of going when reins are released.

THE AIDS

Rider pushes hands forward to completely release contact for two or three strides.
NB This movement is asked for in German tests as

a test of self-carriage. It necessitates a degree of collection so that the horse is sufficiently balanced and engaged to carry himself without the support of the reins.

VARIATIONS TO THE PACES

The purity of the paces was discussed in chapter 4 as one of the primary goals in dressage. In this chapter the paces are discussed as movements *ie* how changes can be made within each pace to the length and type of stride.

FREE WALK ON A LONG REIN

THE AIMS

1 To maintain a light contact, but an allowing one, so the horse has complete freedom to lower and stretch his head and neck. **NB** Free walk on a loose rein is not asked for in tests, but is when the contact is given away completely, so the reins are looped.
2 To take long, purposeful strides – the horse should overtrack.

THE AID

1 Maintain contact with leg and seat to keep the horse walking purposefully forward.
2 Gradually ease the fingers, encouraging the horse to take the rein forward and down.

COMMON FAULTS AND POSSIBLE CORRECTIONS

1 Strides become hurried and short. Use lighter leg and seat aids. Make occasional checks with one rein before releasing again.
2 Strides lack purpose and length (they should overtrack easily). Use sharper leg aids for a few strides, perhaps reinforced with the whip just behind a leg. Use alternate leg aids. Open the fingers to allow the horse to take more rein.
3 Head remains behind the vertical – ensure rein contact is not too strong; needs more work on suppleness.

A free walk. This horse has taken the rein forward and down and is purposeful in his attitude

4 Head and neck do not stretch forward and down but remain horizontal, or horse even lifts the head when reins are released – this shows that the horse is not working 'through' his back, there is tension in the muscles, the 'basics' have not been established. The rider needs to work on the 'scales' of training.

5 Tenses up and breaks into a trot – relax the horse, keep the walk slow. In training make a small circle before freeing the reins to help him let go, and again when taking up the contact. Use of the voice can be helpful in training.

MEDIUM WALK

THE AIMS

1 A 'free' walk with the horse on the bit (head on or just beyond vertical). The rider maintains a light, soft and steady contact with the mouth.

2 The steps are of moderate extension so the horse should overtrack.

3 The steps are regular, unconstrained, even and purposeful.

4 The horse is calm but energetic.

THE AIDS

1 Maintain contact with leg, seat and hand aids to keep horse walking purposefully forward into the contact.

COMMON FAULTS AND POSSIBLE CORRECTIONS

1 Quick short strides – reduce driving aids, use loosening and stretching work mainly at trot to encourage horse to work 'through' back.

2 Lazy strides which do not cover the ground – occasional sharp leg aids, perhaps reinforced with whip; use alternate leg aids, do not apply legs together in rhythm of stride as this has soporific effect.

3 Uneven strides – check for physical problems; also rider may be sitting crooked, or rein contact may be uneven.

4 Loss of sequence, losing four-time marching

A medium walk. The horse is taking a good contact and showing good length of strides

An extended walk. This is a young horse with only moderate extension to his strides. He has taken the rein forward to show a distinct difference in the outline to the medium walk

rhythm – if young horse, try not to walk on the bit during training, walk on a free rein as much as possible. If more advanced, horse needs to learn to let go to become more supple. Lateral work in walk can help.

EXTENDED WALK
THE AIMS
1 The horse stretches out his head and neck while still keeping that light, soft steady contact.
2 The strides are lengthened so they cover as much ground as possible and there is clear overtracking.
3 The steps are regular, unconstrained, even and determined.
4 The horse is calm but energetic.

THE AIDS
1 The rider asks the horse to lengthen his strides with slightly stronger leg aids, but with a gradual build up so they can be reduced quickly if the

horse starts to run or get tense.
2 Push the hands forward to allow him to stretch forwards, but do not lose the contact.

COMMON FAULTS AND POSSIBLE CORRECTIONS
1 As for medium walk.

COLLECTED WALK
THE AIMS
1 The horse is on the bit with his neck raised and arched (head close to the vertical). A light soft steady contact is maintained.
2 The strides are shorter, with the hind feet touching the ground behind, or in the hoofprints of the forefeet (not overtracking). Shortening is achieved through increased flexion of the joints.
3 The steps are regular, even and active, with the hindlegs well engaged and showing good hock action.
4 The horse is calm but energetic.

THE AIDS
1 Series of half halts.

Above left: A collected walk which shows some of the problems of trying to collect a young horse. The strides are shorter but he has restricted the aids and this could easily lead to a loss of regularity. Most trainers do not try to collect the walk until a horse is working at medium level

COMMON FAULTS AND POSSIBLE CORRECTIONS

1 Tense, hurried steps – calm the horse with 'clinging' legs and a light relaxed seat. In training use circles and the voice.

2 Shortens strides but loses activity and the hinds tend to be dragged along – occasional stimulating leg aids reinforced by use of whip; check that rider is not trying to collect by pulling on reins, the reins should only restrain while the hindquarters are activated. The horse is ridden from rear to front for good collection not vice versa.

3 Uneven strides – as for medium.

4 Loss of sequence which, if very bad, turns the walk into a two-time pace. Usually due to not letting go, asking the horse to collect when he is tense and/or before he is not sufficiently supple in his back and joints. Return to basics and do not ask

for collection, or at least not as much and use lateral exercises.

WORKING TROT

1 Maintains a light, soft steady rein contact.

2 As the type of trot in which the untrained horse finds it easiest to maintain balance, it is the closest to his natural/normal trot. The strides are neither so short as in collection nor as long as medium.

3 Goes forward with regular, even elastic steps and good hock action.

4 Works 'through' a soft 'swinging' back.

5 A marked cadence.

THE AIDS

1 Use leg, seat and hand aids to keep horse working 'through' to the hands.

COMMON FAULTS AND POSSIBLE CORRECTIONS

1 Does not swing 'through' the back, but is cramped and stiff – if in sitting trot, go back to rising. Use stretching exercises and circles. May be caused by lifting head and neck without the

corresponding lowering and engaging of hindquarters ie ridden from front to rear to hold the neck up.

2 Tempo changes slowing down and/or speeding up – if due to being restricted by the reins, ask for longer strides with a lighter contact. If being asked too much, so losing balance and hurrying, slow down and reduce the length of the strides.

3 Lack of engagement, stiff hinds – although not asking for collection, it is essential that the hinds generate impulsion with good active flexing. Therefore increase the driving aids, use transitions and half halts to help engagement.

4 Tilting, short in neck and overbending, hollowing and above the bit, unsteady head – if no physical problems, concentrate on establishing the basics.

LENGTHENED STRIDES
THE AIMS
1 Without changing the tempo of the rhythm of the working trot, show about half-a-dozen lengthened strides.

2 The steps are regular, free, unconstrained and even.

3 The impulsion is obvious.

Above centre: This is a rather pleasing working trot although, ideally, there could be a little less weight on the forehand

Above right: A good example of a young horse lengthening his strides

4 The horse remains on the bit.

5 A marked cadence.

THE AIDS
1 As for medium trot, see below.

COMMON PROBLEMS AND POSSIBLE CORRECTIONS
1 Rhythm changes, the strides get quicker ultimately leading to shortening rather than lengthening of strides – half halts, in training return to working trot and try again, build up more engagement and impulsion before asking for lengthened strides.

2 Running onto the forehand – ask for more engagement before giving the aids for lengthening, half halt when lengthening, ensure the rider does not tip forward putting more weight onto the forehand.

3 Stiffening against the aids and hollowing the back – establish the basics, try rising to the trot.

4 Forgeing – young horses which are rather weak and unbalanced often hit their fore shoes with their hinds; this is a fault, but most horses grow out of it if correctly trained, balanced and strengthened.

MEDIUM TROT

THE AIMS

1 While remaining on the bit, the rider allows the head and neck to be lowered slightly, with the head a little further in front of the vertical than in working or collected trot.

2 The strides are of moderate extension.

3 The steps are regular, free, unconstrained and even.

4 The impulsion is obvious.

5 A marked cadence.

THE AIDS

1 The rider applies the driving aids (leg and seat).

2 When the rider feels the extra impulsion coming through the back and poll into his hands, he allows the horse to stretch his head and neck slightly.

3 Half halt as and when necessary to maintain balance and evenness to strides.

COMMON PROBLEMS AND POSSIBLE CORRECTIONS

1 Horse starts to run and hurry – check and start again; build up balance and impulsion, work on a 20 metre circle, lengthen for a few strides, then collect up again, then lengthen again.

2 Falls onto forehand – increase engagement, use more half halts, ensure contact is maintained. Some riders seem to think the aid to lengthen is merely to let the reins go, but the easing of the contact is *preceded*, not followed, by the driving aids and the contact is never given away completely. Use more half halts.

3 Wide behind – usually due to weakness, so spend time on strengthening the hindquarters and getting them more engaged.

4 Irregular strides, one hind takes a different step to the other hind (sometimes a foreleg although more rare) – check for physical problems, ill-fitting saddle, crooked riding, uneven rein contact.

5 Uneven strides – usually due to rider asking for more lengthening than horse can maintain, so he loses his balance and shortens up for a few strides. Ask for less and keep him balanced.

6 Loss of roundness, horse hollows/stiffens his back, sometimes a tendency to flick the forelegs – needs more engagement, more work to get him working 'through' his back and more surely on the bit. Lengthen in rising trot.

EXTENDED TROT

THE AIMS

1 Horse lengthens his frame, slightly stretching out his head and neck, remaining lightly on the bit and not leaning on it.

2 The strides are lengthened to their utmost as a result of great impulsion from the hind quarters.

3 Maintains cadence.

4 Forefeet should touch the ground on the spots towards which they are pointing ie no flicking of forelegs.

THE AID

1 As for medium trot, but asking a little more with the driving aids, allowing a little more with the hands.

COMMON PROBLEMS AND POSSIBLE CORRECTIONS

1 1–6 as for medium trot (see above).

NB Any flicking of the forelegs becomes more pronounced in the extended trot, and is usually the result of not being worked to a true contact but having a rather high head carriage and light contact and the back is rather tight. If flicking starts, go back to the basics.

COLLECTED TROT

THE AIMS

1 While remaining on the bit the neck is raised and arched, with the head close to the vertical.

2 The strides are shorter than in any other trot.

3 The hinds are well engaged, the hocks well flexed.

4 The forehand is slightly higher and lighter. The shoulders have more freedom to move with ease in any direction. The horse is more mobile.

The medium trot in which the horse is clearly showing the moment of suspension

The extended trot in which the steps and frame are longer than in the medium trot

The collected trot in which the strides become shorter, higher and more engaged

Above: Extending the trot across the diagonal to show good freedom and self carriage

Below: Collecting the trot but losing the self carriage. This horse needs to step under more with his hind legs to keep his forehand light

Above: A young horse in working trot. He is showing good carriage but is not yet able to show engagement, activity of the hind legs and lightness of forehand that the trained horse is producing in the collected trot below

5 The impulsion is obvious.
6 A marked cadence.

THE AIDS

1 Series of half halts, the rider stretching his back upwards.

COMMON PROBLEMS AND POSSIBLE CORRECTIONS

1 Steps flat, hocks stiff and there is a lack of cadence – apply driving aids to ask horse to go forwards more and restore a swing to the trot.
2 Short in neck, behind the bit, steps short but hinds not engaged – rider is probably collecting from in front to behind, not vice versa, and is using too much hand. More use of legs and seat to ask to step into the bit, and lighten rein contact, especially after each half halt so can come into better self carriage.
3 Slows down into passage like floating trot – ask to go forward, restore faster tempo, and when ask for more collection go forward again if starts to slow down the rhythm.

WORKING CANTER
THE AIMS

1 Maintains a light, soft steady contact.
2 Similarly to the trot, it is the canter in which the untrained horse finds it easiest to maintain balance. The strides are neither so short as in collection or as long as in medium.
3 Goes forward with even, light cadenced strides and good hock action.

THE AIDS

1 Use leg, seat and hands to establish and maintain a balanced rhythmical canter.

COMMON PROBLEMS AND POSSIBLE CORRECTIONS

1 Hinds stiff and dragged along; although not asking for collection, active hindquarters are needed to produce the important spring to the pace – transitions in and out of and within the canter, positive working from behind to a soft elastic contact; check not being held back by pulling hand.

2 Loss of sequence, deteriorating into a four-time canter – corrections as in 1, more activity, more spring.
3 Disunited canter – return to trot and establish correct lead.
4 Hollowing and stiffening of the back – more engagement as in 1, stretching and suppling exercises, more surely onto the bit.
5 Quarters in, *ie* is not straight – work more positively forward, shoulder fore positioning (p97), in training counter canter work (p88), check rider is not sitting crooked.
6 On forehand/croup high – transitions, more half halts, check rider is upright and not tipping forward.
7 Tilting/short in neck and overbending/hollowing and above the bit/unsteady head – if no physical problems concentrate on establishing the basics, riding the horse up from behind into a steady, even elastic rein contact.

LENGTHENED STRIDES

As for working trot except that there is no forgeing in canter.

MEDIUM CANTER
THE AIMS

1 Remains on the bit when the head and neck are lowered slightly so the head reaches a little further in front of the vertical than in collected.
2 The strides are of moderate extension.
3 The steps are unconstrained, balanced, free and even.
4 Hoofbeats three-time with clear moment of suspension.
5 The impulsion is obvious with the horse working 'through' the back.

THE AIDS

1 The rider asks for the longer strides with the driving aids (leg and seat).
2 When the rider feels the extra impulsion coming through the back and poll into his hands he allows with his hands so the horse can lengthen and stretch his head and neck slightly.
3 Half halt as and when necessary to retain balance and evenness of strides.

A working canter when the strides are neither so long as in the medium pace, nor as short as in collected canter

The medium canter showing more engagement, a higher carriage and longer steps than in the working canter

The extended canter. This horse is showing good activity of the hind legs but not enough difference in the length of frame and strides from medium canter to be a good extended pace

This sequence shows different stages in the canter when the rider has asked for an extension across the diagonal. The length of the steps and outline would be good for a medium canter but not enough for an extended canter

Left: This horse is collecting well, stepping under the weight, and is lighter in the forehand than the horse shown in the following two photographs

Note the uphill appearance of the horse on the left, just after the moment of suspension, and the downhill appearance on the right, just before the moment of suspension

Centre and right: As in the trot shown on page 80, this horse is finding it difficult to engage and shorten and produce the collection without losing self carriage. Allowance should be made for the fact that these photographs were taken at a stage in the canter sequence when the horse tips forward

COMMON PROBLEMS AND POSSIBLE CORRECTIONS

1 Hurried, short strides – stop driving, re-establish working/collected canter and start again, build up balance and impulsion, work on a 20 metre circle lengthening for a few strides, then collecting up, and then try lengthening again.

2 Falls onto forehand/croup high – increase engagement. Ensure contact is maintained, do not lengthen by letting reins go because the easing of the contact should be preceded by, not followed by, the driving aids, and the contact is never given away completely. Use more half halts.

3 Tempo varies – usually due to rider asking for more lengthening than horse can maintain so loses balance and rhythm; ask for less and keep him balanced.

4 Quarters in – ensure is in shoulder fore position (see p97) or at least straight before applying driving aids. Keep 'thinking' shoulder-fore aids when in medium canter. In training, lengthen in counter canter (see p88) across diagonal or on long side of arena.

5 Hollowing and stiffening of the back – more engagement, more work to get horse working 'through' his back and more surely on the bit.

EXTENDED CANTER
THE AIMS

1 Remains on the bit, does not lean into it when lowering and extending his head and neck, the head reaching beyond the vertical.

2 The strides cover as much ground as possible.

3 Steps balanced, unconstrained, even and unhurried.

4 Hoofbeats clearly three-time with suspension pronounced.

5 The impulsion is obvious with the horse working 'through' the back.

THE AIDS

1 As for medium canter, with stronger driving aids and slightly more allowing with the hands.

COMMON PROBLEMS AND POSSIBLE CORRECTIONS

1 As for medium canter (see above).

The self-carriage has been lost in this canter

COLLECTED CANTER
THE AIMS

1 As for collected trot (see p78).

THE AIDS

1 As for collected trot (see p82).

COMMON PROBLEMS AND POSSIBLE CORRECTIONS

1 Short in neck, steps short but not engaged – collection from front to hindquarters, not vice versa, too much use of rein. Ride forwards, establish engagement and collect by using seat and legs, and frequent lightening of rein contact, especially after each half halt.

2 Four-time canter – corrections as in 1.

3 Nods head in rhythm with the beat – lacks impulsion and engagement to maintain balance. Ride forward and establish more engagement.

4 Quarters in – straighten with shoulder fore positioning and riding forward.

5 Too much bend in neck, falling onto outside shoulder – more outside rein to control bend, less inside rein. Shoulder fore positioning. Counter flexion to help bring shoulders in front of hind quarters.

REIN BACK

THE AIMS

1 To establish a halt before the rein back.

2 Horse remains on the bit, ready to move forward and does so immediately the rein back is finished.

3 The legs move in diagonal pairs, but with the fore-leg of the pair being lifted and set down an instant before the hind.

4 The joints flex distinctly so the limbs are clearly lifted and not dragged backwards.

5 The horse should go backwards in a straight line and without spreading his hindlegs.

6 The horse should go backwards without hesitation or rushing.

THE AIDS

1 After a good halt has been established the rider draws back his legs a little behind the girth and applies them, but as the horse goes to step forward he meets the rider's non-allowing hands (no pulling back) and steps backwards rather than forwards.

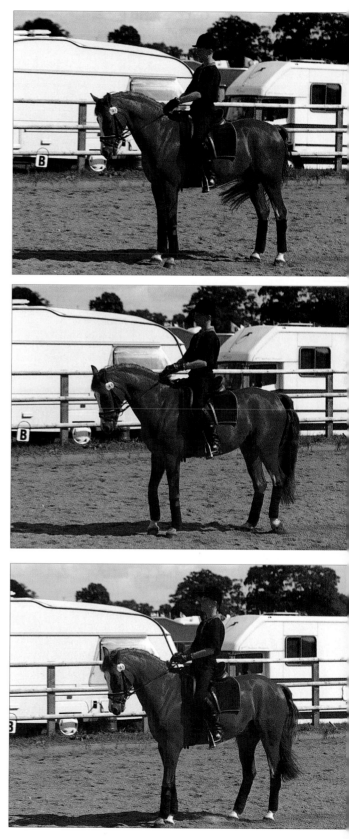

The rein back: (above) the rider is using the hands too much and the horse is overbending. In the sequence on the right the rider is not pulling back, the horse keeps a good outline but the steps are rather short

2 As the horse steps back the reins can be lightened but without losing contact.

3 For young horses and those with sensitive backs it is usually more effective to lighten the seat, to put more weight onto the thighs.

COMMON PROBLEMS AND POSSIBLE CORRECTIONS

1 Horse resists going back – often due to halting with the hindquarters behind him. Establish a better halt before asking for rein back.

2 Hollowing in rein back – usual cause is the rider pulling the horse backwards with the reins; establish better aids, and work on the basics. Rider might be sitting too heavily.

3 Rushes backwards, behind the bit – only ask for a few strides at a time and then ride firmly forwards into the bit. Use the voice and ensure the horse is relaxed before asking for the rein back.

4 Steps to one side when reining back – ensure rider's legs are in a supportive position. Ensure rein pressure is even; if there is a stronger feel in rein on opposite side to the hind which steps out this will aggravate the problem. Rein back with a wall or fence on the side to which he tries to curl in. Work to strengthen quarters, particularly on side to which he deviates.

5 Drags the hinds – usually due to lack of engagement; work on strengthening quarters and establishing halt with quarters well engaged before rein back.

6 Wide behind – try to establish more engagement before asking for rein back, as 4.

VARIATIONS TO THE CANTER

COUNTER CANTER

THE AIMS

1 To canter on a left circle/turn with right leg leading and vice versa.

2 To maintain flexion at the poll to the side of the leading leg.

3 To maintain slight bend around the rider's inside leg (the side of the leading leg), but although the

The counter canter shown with rather a big bend in the neck which is throwing the weight onto the right shoulder

horse does not bend to the line of the circle/turn, he should remain on one track, his hindquarters following the forelegs and not swinging to the outside of the circle.

4 All the requirements of the canter are maintained *ie* cadence, impulsion, three-time beat etc.

TRAINING EXERCISES

1 Start by making a very shallow (about 3 metres) loop away from the long side.

2 Half circle back to long side, keep in counter canter until just before short side then transition in trot. As he improves, progress to going around short side in counter canter. Return to easier exercises if he changes the leading leg.

The counter canter shown by quite an advanced horse who is finding it easy and is retaining self carriage

THE AIDS

1 The same aids as when asking for a particular canter lead, *ie* in counter canter on right lead, maintain flexion to right with inside leg and soft inside rein, maintain balance, amount of bend and speed with supportive outside rein, while outside leg is held in a supportive manner behind the girth which discourages a flying change.

COMMON PROBLEMS AND POSSIBLE CORRECTIONS

1 Loss of impulsion, tendency towards four-time canter – before going into turn, increase engagement and impulsion.

2 Hindquarters drift to one side – keep in shoulder fore position.

3 Changes leg – in training probably asking for too sheer a turn for stage of training. It is important to introduce counter canter progressively, only asking for shallow loops at first, and building up degree of difficulty as horse progresses. Check rider is not crooked; keep balanced and with that supportive outside leg firmly on the horse's side.

4 Uneven strides, either quickening or becoming

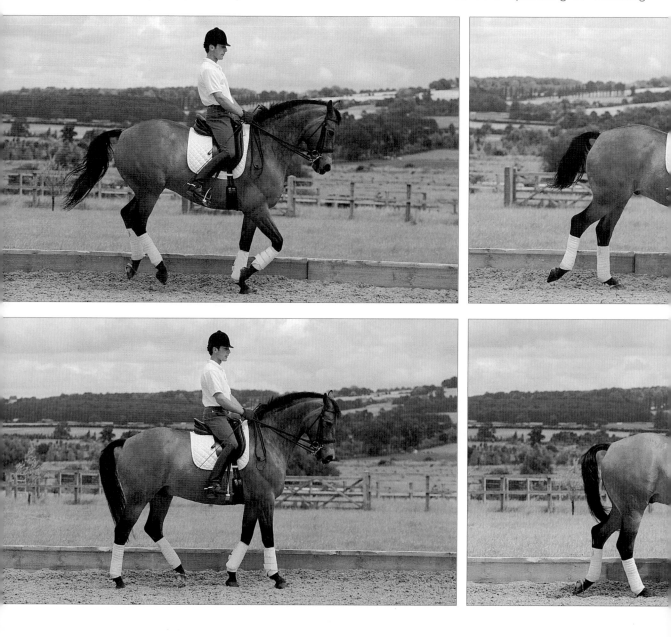

laboured – usually due to loss of balance; increase engagement, half halts, go back to a less sheer turn.

SIMPLE CHANGE OF LEG

THE AIMS

1 A direct transition from canter to walk, with all the above prerequisites of a downward transition (p67).

2 Two or three steps of a true walk.

3 A direct transition from walk to canter on the other lead with all the prerequisites of an upward transition (p67).

A sequence showing the simple change of leg from left to right. In the first two photographs the horse is in counter canter and in the third and fourth (top right and bottom left) the rider has applied the aids and the horse is establishing the walk. In the fifth photograph the rider is asking for a right flexion before the strike off and in the last picture the horse is about to strike off into the canter stride.
(The first two photographs are not part of the sequence but they do show the canter on the left leg)

NB In some national tests simple changes are used when transitions may still be progressive. This means that one or two trot strides may be shown in both transitions. In some tests more than three steps of walk are required.

THE AIDS

1 As for transitions, see p67.

COMMON PROBLEMS AND POSSIBLE CORRECTIONS

1 As for transitions 1, 2, 3 and 4, see p67.
2 Walk not clearly established – in training, walk for more than two or three strides and gradually reduce number as movement becomes more established.

3 Walk loses sequence – usually due to tension, too strong hand aids. Train with progressive transitions and gradually reduce the number of trot strides.

4 Tightens in walk and against aids to canter – leg yield in walk steps (to left when strike off is to right and vice versa)

FLYING CHANGE OF LEG
THE AIMS

1 In a good forward collected canter (**NB** degree of collection tends to be slightly less than in other movements), to change cleanly during the movement of suspension in the canter to opposite lead with both fore and hind legs at the same time.
2 To remain light, calm and straight.

A flying change on to the right lead and with the rider positioning himself clearly to the right

3 To keep same balance, rhythm and impulsion throughout, even if the changes are in a series, *ie* every fourth, third, second or every stride.

4 The change has 'expression', *ie* is free, bold and cadenced.

THE AIDS

1 Prepare – as for all movements – with half halts.

2 Establish a slight flexion to direction of the lead required.

3 Change position of seat and legs to come in line with new flexion. The rider's old outside leg comes forward, and old inside slides back and nudges horse just as the forehand starts to rise into the moment of suspension. The timing of these aids is crucial as the horse only has the ability to change correctly during the moment of suspension. The aid must be given just before it, just before the horse lifts into the air.

TRAINING EXERCISES

1 Counter canter on a circle and ask for the change.

2 Travers on a circle, straighten and ask for the change.

3 Half pass, as reach track straighten and ask for the change.

4 Half circle and as return to the track ask for the change.

COMMON PROBLEMS AND POSSIBLE CORRECTIONS

1 The horse only changes in front – usually due to horse not having had sufficient training – there is therefore insufficient engagement and strength in his hindquarters. Return to establishing basics – until a horse is able to perform simple changes with ease and quality, is able to collect his canter and keep straight, he is not ready to learn changes.

2 Change is late behind *ie* horse changes behind one or more strides after the front leg – usually due to not being sufficiently on the aids – go back to basics. Lack of engagement and collection before the change; use more half halts, use more exercises to assist engagement just before the change *ie* simple changes, half pass, use a very definite outside leg aid and it can be reinforced by a tap with the whip.

3 Change is not 'through', the new leading hind does not come forward sufficiently in the change – corrections as for 2 above.

4 Change is not straight, swings hindquarters to the side – when establishing new flexion ask for a shoulder fore positioning. Take care not to give too strong an aid with the new outside leg. Ride forward more just before and during the change.

5 Change short and stiff – improve the canter so horse working 'through' back. Make the horse rounder. Clear half halt before riding more forward and asking for a bolder change.

6 Tense changes – keep going back to basics, as tension is often because the horse is finding it difficult to change *ie* he is not truly on the aids, does not have enough engagement or straightness; work on simple changes, so he understands the aids clearly. Use the voice and reward him well after each correct change, return to walk on free rein after each change.

7 Change is croup high – the horse is lacking in engagement. Work on the canter to improve this; he must be able to collect without losing cadence and spring.

6

Lateral Movements

In lateral work the horse moves sideways as well as forwards. The lateral movements are not just an end in themselves as movements, but are a means to improving the horse's way of going, the rhythm, suppleness, connection, impulsion, straightness and collection. At no time must the desire to achieve a certain lateral positioning override the need to maintain the purity of the gaits, impulsion and submission. Avoid asking for so much bend or sideways movement that the quality of the paces, impulsion and/or cadence is lost.

Sometimes lateral work is referred to as two-track work because the horse is moving on two or more tracks, and is no longer straight when the hind feet move along the same track as corresponding forefeet. **NB** lateral work can include three- (shoulder in) or four-track (travers) movements too.

LEG YIELDING

THE AIMS

1 Horse is straight, except for a slight flexion at the poll away from the direction in which he is moving (to the inside).
2 The horse's legs pass and cross in front of the outside legs.

THE AIDS

1 Establish just enough flexion at the poll with the inside rein and leg to see the horse's eyebrow and nostril on the inside. Contact on the inside rein should be kept light.
2 Rider to maintain central and balanced position but transfer a little more weight onto the inside seat bone and stirrup.
3 Ask horse to step sideways with inside leg just behind the girth.
4 Support with the outside rein, so does not fall onto outside shoulder.
5 Support with outside leg and use if necessary to stop horse rushing sideways.

TRAINING EXERCISES

Most riders start teaching leg yielding in walk.
1 Complete a half circle which establishes that slight flexion to the inside, and as complete half circle apply the aids for the leg yield, ie half circle to left, leg yield to right.
2 As end of the short side of the school is reached keep the horse pointing towards the wall fence of the long side of the school and apply the aids

Leg yielding with too much bend to the left so that the weight is falling onto the right shoulder, making it difficult to move fluently sideways

Leg yielding to the right in a good balance with just a small flexion to the left

for the leg yield with the horse's head to the wall and with his body at an angle of about 35 degrees to it.

COMMON PROBLEMS AND POSSIBLE CORRECTIONS

1 Excessive bend and falling onto outside shoulder – small checks with outside rein, less inside rein.
2 Loss of impulsion, cadence, etc – ask to go more forwards, less sideways. Work on basics.
3 Does not step sideways – check rider not losing position and collapsing, must keep both seat bones in the saddle and think forwards, not too much sideways. Use taps with whip, or even occasional use of spur to make more sensitive to aid to step sideways.

SHOULDER FORE
THE AIMS

1 The horse is very slightly bent along his whole body to the inside so he is no longer looking straight ahead. The rider can just see his eye and nostril.
2 The horse's forelegs are brought slightly to the inside so that the inside hind steps between them and the outside straight ahead in the direction of the outside shoulder.

THE AIDS

1 As for shoulder in below, but ask for less angle.

COMMON PROBLEMS AND POSSIBLE CORRECTIONS

1 As for shoulder in below.

Leg yielding from behind showing good crossing and a pretty upright position from the rider

Shoulder fore with the shoulders having been taken off the track but not as much as in the shoulder in

SHOULDER IN
THE AIMS

1 Horse is slightly bent around the rider's inside leg so he is looking away from the direction in which he is moving.

2 The horse's forehand is brought to the inside of the track so the inside foreleg passes and crosses in front of the outside foreleg. The inside hind leg is placed under the body and in front of the outside hind which entails lowering the inside hip and therefore some degree of collection.

3 The angle to the school should be about 30 degrees.

NB Usually this movement is on three tracks, but it can be done on four tracks when the horse has to be at a greater angle to the track.

THE AIDS

1 Prepare – as always – with the half halt and then apply the aids to turn horse off the track, *ie* turn shoulders, transfer weight to inside, use inside leg on the girth, soften contact and indicate flexion with inside rein.

2 As soon as he turns, restrain with outside rein to stop him from moving off the track.

3 The outside rein then controls the bend, the position and the outside shoulder.

4 Inside leg used to keep bend and energy.

5 Outside leg used further behind than the inside to support and stop quarters falling out.

6 Inside rein contact should be light and elastic.

TRAINING EXERCISES

Most riders start teaching the shoulder in in walk and progress to the trot.

1 After short side, or a small volte which establishes the flexion, ask for shoulder in.

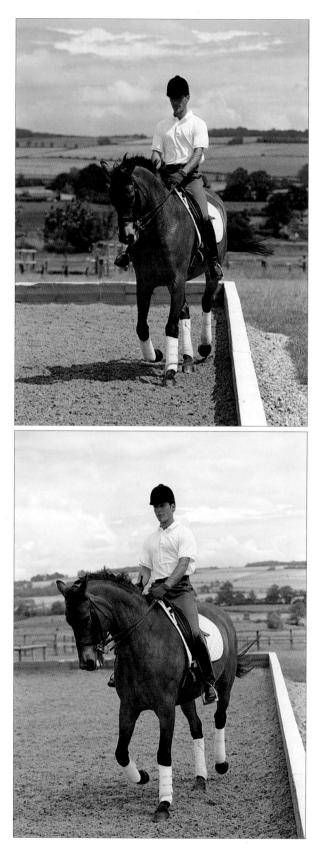

Top left and right: Shoulder in with a good balance and showing the positioning with different diagonals in the air

Below left: Shoulder in with too much angle so that the inside hind does not step forward and under the weight but just sideways, as in leg yielding

Below right: Shoulder in with too much neck bend so the weight tends to fall towards the left shoulder

COMMON PROBLEMS AND POSSIBLE CORRECTIONS

1 Falling onto outside shoulder – often due to excessive use of inside rein. Reduce inside rein aids and use more outside rein.

2 More bend in neck than in body – corrections as 1.

3 Quarters swing out – stronger support from outside leg; take care that not due to too strong inside rein or inside leg too far back.

4 Head tilting – can be due to uneven rein contact, and/or not stepping through evenly with hind legs, both causes require more serious work on basics, and/or check that rider is balanced and not collapsing a hip (see chapter 2, p27).

5 Loss of impulsion, submission – if possible, return to circle or straight line as soon as this occurs, and establish basics more firmly before re-applying aids for the movement. Do not ask for so much angle, and if still losing impulsion/submission, then horse needs more long-term work on the basics before training for this movement. To be done correctly, shoulder in does require some degree of collection and in most cases this is only achieved with a young horse after good work on the other basics for a year or more.

TRAVERS

THE AIMS

1 To slightly bend the horse around the rider's inside leg, but unlike the shoulder in, this will be in the direction in which he is going.

2 The horse moves on four tracks (*ie* if viewed from the front, four feet can be seen), with both outside legs passing and crossing in front of their respective inside legs.

3 The horse should move along the long side or centre line at an angle of about 30 degrees.

4 As in other movements there should be no loss of rhythm, impulsion or submission, nor should the purity of the paces be impaired.

THE AIDS

1 Prepare with a half halt.

2 Establish flexion with inside leg and rein and positioning of the seat (*ie* keeping shoulders parallel with those of the horse).

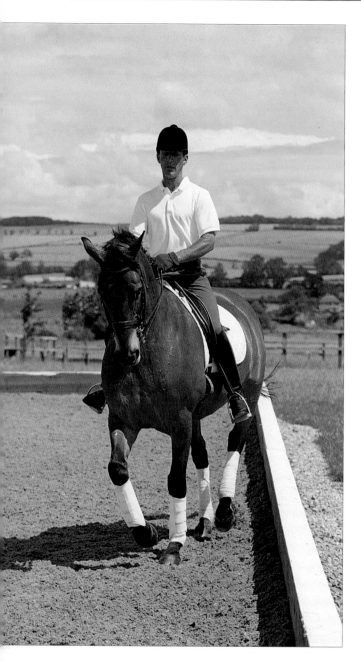

Renvers in a pretty good position but with a slight tendency to tilt instead of flex. The left ear is a little higher than the right

3 Outside leg used further behind the girth guides the quarters to the inside of the track and helps to bend the horse around the rider's inside leg.

4 The outside hand is supportive, helping balance, speed and amount of bend.

5 Inside leg remains the base around which horse is bent, and is supportive unless needed to liven the pace and stimulate impulsion.

TRAINING EXERCISES

Most teach the horse to understand the aids in walk.

1 Small volte, and as return to long side, guide hindquarters to step sideways with aids as above.

2 As in 1, but start after second turn on short side of school.

3 On a 20 metre circle, apply the aids for travers.

COMMON PROBLEMS AND POSSIBLE CORRECTIONS

1 Horse is not evenly bent around inside leg, but has too much bend in neck and too little in body; usually most of this bend is just in front of the withers – lighten inside rein, increase use of outside rein and inside leg.

2 Sluggish to outside leg aids, and reluctant to step sideways – reinforce with use of stick by outside leg. Make horse more reactive to lateral aids by going back to simpler movements ie leg yield.

3 Losing impulsion – check not at too great an angle for stage of training ie thinking too much sideways, not enough forwards. Increase the liveliness of the inside leg aids.

4 Irregular, usually inside hind that takes a shorter step – often caused by too strong an inside rein on that side, or rider sitting crooked.

5 Tilting head, resisting – as in shoulder in, but usually means more serious work on the basics.

RENVERS

THE AIMS

1 Aims as for 'Travers' except the tail, not the head, is to the long side or centre line.

THE AIDS

1 As for 'Travers'.

TRAINING EXERCISES

1 Down centre line, small circle then on returning to centre line renvers to left if completed a left circle, right if a right one.

2 Shoulder in and then very gradually change the bend to establish renvers.

NB Renvers is more difficult than travers and best taught after the travers is well established.

HALF PASS

THE AIMS

1 This is a variation of the travers and is performed on a diagonal, the horse moving with the fore-hand slightly in advance of the hindquarters, but only just, as the horse should be nearly parallel to the long sides.

2 As in travers, the horse should be bent around the inside leg of the rider, with its outside legs passing and crossing in front of its inside legs.

3 A correct smooth bend so that a shoulder does not protrude and reduce freedom and mobility to the shoulders.

4 Good engagement of the inside hind in particular so impulsion can be maintained.

5 As in other movements, there should be no loss of rhythm, impulsion, submission or purity of the paces.

THE AIDS

1 These are very similar to those for the travers except for the start, when after the preparatory half halt the horse can be ridden into a few strides of shoulder fore to ensure the shoulders are slightly ahead of the hindquarters as he is guided off the track, and forward and sideways across the diagonal.

2 The strength of the aids will have to be adjusted according to the reactions of the horse, as the aim is to keep him on that diagonal line, with the nose just ahead of the inside shoulder, which in its turn is just ahead of the horse's inside hip.

3 The bend to the way of going is established with the inside leg and rein, and the inside rein contact should remain light after indicating direction. The inside leg supports the bend but has to be used

Travers with good positioning – the horse's face is directed down the track

more energetically if there is any loss of impulsion or if the inside shoulder gets too far ahead.

4 The outside leg asks for the sideways action, and if the quarters start to lead its aids should be reduced in strength.

5 The outside rein is supportive, controlling the amount of bend around the inside leg, the speed, balance, and positioning of the outside shoulder.

TRAINING EXERCISES

Ensure shoulder in and travers are established before starting. It can be practised at first in walk.

1 10 metre half circle then back to the track in half pass.

2 Shoulder in then half pass.

3 Leg yield from outside track towards centre line and return in half pass.

When teaching a half pass, most horses will find it difficult to maintain it correctly for more than half-a-dozen strides. As soon as the correct position/impulsion/submission has been lost then either straighten the horse and ride him forward for a few strides, turn him into a circle or into a few steps of shoulder in before re-applying the aids for half pass. Do not keep attempting half pass when the quality of the way of going has been lost.

COMMON PROBLEMS AND POSSIBLE CORRECTIONS

1 Quarters leading – guide the forehand ahead with outside rein and reduce the pushing with outside leg. Ensure clear shoulder in position before half pass is started.

2 Loss of impulsion and cadence – often due to 1 and therefore use same corrections. Also caused by rider not using enough inside leg, too much inside rein, and/or losing his balanced position.

Top l to r: A half pass in sequence. Ideally, the rider's weight should be more to his right, more central and in the direction of the movement

Bottom left: A well balanced half pass but the horse could show a little more bend

Centre: Half pass showing no bend and the rider is not looking in the direction of the movement

Right: Half pass with the rider using too much inside rein and producing too much bend in the neck

Restore impulsion and cadence on a single track and then re-try half pass.

3 Too much bend in the neck; usually most of it is at the wither – more positive use of outside rein to limit bend, less use of inside rein.

4 Irregular, usually on inside hind – too much use of inside rein, rider sitting crooked, physical problem.

5 Quarters trailing – stronger use of outside leg to push quarters over and of outside rein to stop forehand getting too far ahead.

6 Head tilting – can be due to uneven rein contact or to not stepping through evenly with both hinds. Both reasons are usually best corrected by returning to single-track work on the basics, then progressively working towards half pass by establishing good shoulder in and travers and then starting half pass in its easiest form, *ie* asking for very little crossing.

NB In half pass in particular it is very difficult for the rider to stay in balance, and any loss of straightness will make it very difficult for the horse to keep his balance and perform a good half pass. Especially when first learning it can help the rider to maintain an upright position, and not to interfere with the horse, if the half pass is done in rising trot. When this is successful, try sitting, but as soon as the rider loses balance return to rising for a few strides. The position of the rider is crucial so he must stay upright, turned in line with the horse's shoulders and looking through the horse's ears which are directed towards the marker where aiming to return to the track.

PIROUETTE
THE AIM

1 To turn through 180 degrees with the forehand moving round the hindquarters and on a circle of a radius equal to the horse's length.

2 The forefeet and the outside hind foot move around the inside hind foot – which is the pivot – returning to the same spot or slightly in front of it each time it has been lifted.

3 The horse is slightly bent in the direction in which he is turning, remaining on the bit with a light contact and the poll the highest point.

4 Turn should be smooth, and the rhythm – the tempo and correct sequence should be maintained.

5 The horse should not move backwards or sideways.

6 The inside hind must be lifted and returned to the ground in the same rhythm as the outside hind.

The pirouette can be performed at the walk, piaffe and canter. At the walk it is through 180 degrees (half pirouette), and the piaffe and canter pirouettes

can be more – 360 degrees (pirouette) or even two or three complete turns (double or treble pirouettes) – but pirouettes at these two paces are more advanced than the ground covered in this book. The walk pirouette only is discussed below.

THE AIDS

1 Half halt.

2 Inside leg and hand used to establish a slight bend.

3 Outside leg behind the girth asks horse to start turning.

4 Inside leg used to maintain activity and encourage inside hind to be lifted in the rhythm of the walk.

5 Outside rein limits bend and tendency to step forward.

6 Rider must stay in balance ie turning his shoulders so they remain parallel to those of the horse, and turning his hips to keep his weight to the inside.

TRAINING EXERCISES

1 Start with half circles, gradually reducing their diameter and asking horse to return to the track in half pass rather than on one track. Make the half circle smaller until it is a half pirouette.

2 Travers on a half circle and progressively reduce diameter over a number of training sessions until it becomes a pirouette.

COMMON PROBLEMS AND POSSIBLE CORRECTIONS

1 A hind leg does not lift for a stride or more and horse swivels around on it, ie stuck – return to pirouettes of larger radius, more energetic use of rider's inside leg, not too strong use of inside rein.

2 Quarters swing out – firmer use of outside leg, not too strong use of inside rein, think sideways as give the aids, check weight is not drifting to outside.

3 Hindlegs cross over, step sideways – think more forwards as give the aids.

4 Bend is lost – practise larger pirouettes in travers on a circle.

5 Steps back – too strong rein aids, think more forwards.

6 Too large – this is not a serious fault in the early stages, it is much more important to keep up the true sequence of the walk steps.

A sequence of the walk pirouette showing good clear positioning and the rider staying in a good balance. The photograph on the extreme right shows a walk pirouette with a more advanced horse which has more collection and higher carriage

Training Programmes and Methods

Chapters 4 (The Basics), 5 (One Track Movements) and 6 (Lateral Movements) should give the rider a clear idea of the goals, and as discussed before in chapter 2 (The Rider), knowing what you want to achieve, the requirements for the basics and movements, what they look and feel like are the biggest help in the training. Riders must know how they want their horses to go, and must keep steering towards those objectives.

The chart on p108 is aimed at giving a very rough guide to the stages of training, and when the movements might be introduced. The speed with which a horse progresses from one stage to the next will depend on the maturity and talents of the horse, and the ability and experience of the rider, but if the first stage begins after the horse is backed, it is rare for it to take less than one year.

In the preparatory stage, the basic 'scales' are usually introduced in the order given, but cannot be isolated or worked on separately after their introduction, as they affect and improve each other. At this first stage, too, the movements are attached to a particular basic 'scale' as the one most likely to improve it, but above this level movements have an effect on most of the scales. Any attachment to one rather than another is too great a simplification.

Basically the chart intends to give the rider some guidelines along which to make his plans. Although arena work is usually the fastest way of progressing training, there are enormous advantages to providing plenty of variety to the work which will help to keep the horse fresh mentally and leads to better all round physical development.

I PREPARATORY STAGE

BASIC	AIM	MOVEMENT
Rhythm	Balanced to obtain a regular pronounced rhythm. Not hurried, not sluggish.	Large circles, working trot and later working canter; development of half halt.
Suppleness	Swings through the back, seeks the hand, stretching forward and down if rider allows horse to champ the rein out of the hands.	Figure of eight, free walk. on a long rein, serpentines, 'champ the reins out of the the hands'.
Connection	Working forwards to a consistent elastic contact.	Asking with legs (and seat) to work forwards into the hands, progressive transitions.
Impulsion	In front of the leg, has the desire and engagement to go forwards with elastic steps.	Lengthening strides, transitions (particularly walk to trot and trot to walk).
Straightness	Takes a contact on both reins.	Working forwards boldly without running, circles.

2 PREPARING FOR NOVICE TESTS

BASIC	AIM	MOVEMENT
Rhythm	To improve balance so can maintain rhythm in 12–15m circles and lateral work	More direct transitions, halt from trot, walk to canter, medium walk, leg yielding, developing lengthened strides into medium trot, and canter, shoulder fore, smaller circles, counter canter loops, rein back.
Suppleness	Improve suppleness and tone to muscles.	
Connection	Working onto the bit with self carriage.	
Impulsion	Hindlegs start to carry not just push.	
Straightness	Hind feet stepping along same tracks as forefeet on circle and straight lines.	

3 PREPARING FOR ELEMENTARY TESTS

BASIC	AIM	MOVEMENT
Rhythm		Direct transitions and through two paces, simple changes, develop medium into extended paces, counter canter in circles, collected trot and canter, voltes, walk pirouettes, shoulder-in.
Suppleness	Develop acceptance and sensitivity to aids without resistance.	
Connection	Develop self carriage and lightness.	
Impulsion	Increase ability to shorten and lengthen strides. Increase carrying power of hindquarters.	
Straightness		
Collection		

4 PREPARING FOR MEDIUM TESTS

BASIC	AIM	MOVEMENT
Rhythm	Further improvement and development of aims in elementary programme.	Direct transitions and to include canter to halt and rein back to trot and canter, travers, renvers, half pass, collected walk, flying changes, stroking the horse's neck.
Suppleness		
Connection		
Impulsion		
Straightness		
Collection		

HACKING OUT

Riding out in the country is useful to keep the horse mentally fresh, to improve his physique by hardening up his legs and developing his muscles and by furthering the basics – rhythm, suppleness, connection, impulsion and straightness – which can be worked on when hacking, cantering, galloping and jumping.

With the young horse that has just been broken, hacking out is a wonderful way of getting him thinking forward. Tackling small turns in an enclosed school is difficult for him when he is weak and struggling to find his balance with the weight of the rider, and therefore should only be done for short sessions. Walking on roads and tracks, preferably with an older horse to keep him company, and trotting and cantering wherever the going is good enough, is less demanding physically and more stimulating mentally.

Hill work is an excellent way to develop the horse's muscles, especially those important back muscles; if these hills are on the roads, again, keep to

Hacking out, particularly in company, helps to keep horses mentally fresh and physically fit

the walk or slow trot. If there are hills with sandy tracks, or in fields when the going is good, they can be tackled at a trot or canter.

If it is possible to hack across open country with good going, as the horse matures start practising some of the movements. Ask the horse for a little lengthening and shortening in the trot, to step sideways away from the inside leg, and later to start shoulder in.

With horses that are a little further on in their training – at novice level and above – hacking is no longer so important for building up strength, but it is still an important means of revitalisation and giving variety to their work.

CANTERING

An important aspect of training dressage horses is getting them fit enough to be able to do the work with ease, and to always keep them thinking forward.

Cantering on good going is an excellent means of obtaining these objectives. If the horse is a little lazy then it helps to canter another horse alongside. If the horse is high spirited then canter him on his own at a steady pace, and if possible over a longish distance so there is time to settle into a rhythm.

The cantering should be done on good going. Like the roads, if the surface is hard then it jars the horse, with the likely loss of elasticity of his steps. Try to find a sandy track without stones, and one that is not too deep. Grass is ideal when it is neither too hard nor too soft. Racehorse trainers' gallops are excellent, and many of these are available for hire.

Cantering will do most good if the horse can be settled into a steady rhythm, and if he remains on a soft, elastic contact. He should not be allowed to fall onto his forehand, but work with his hind legs well engaged and taking springy strides. Even when out of the arena the basics should be maintained.

Lungeing is an important part of the training as long as it is done well and the horse helped to establish rhythm, suppleness, connection and, as he advances, impulsion and straightness

Young horses who have just been broken in need to learn to adjust to carrying the weight of the rider in the canter, and it is usually easier for them to do this in big fields or along sandy tracks, rather than in the enclosed space of a school.

LUNGEING

Lungeing is one of the best aids to dressage training. It has numerous benefits, but one of the most important is to enable the trainer to see what the horse is doing. He can see whether the horse is moving straight, that the hind legs do not fall to the inside or outside; see his natural outline, and judge at what tempo the horse shows off his paces to their best advantage. This is one of the crucial features in training, establishing a trot which is neither so slow that the horse in inactive, not so fast that he starts to run and quicken and finds it difficult to let go. For each horse, and frequently for each horse at different stages, the tempo will be different, but there is always one tempo which will make the most of his trot and show off this pace to its

best advantage. This can be assessed on the lunge.

A second benefit is to establish respect and obedience. On the lunge the horse can be taught to go forward and to change paces at the command of the trainer.

The third benefit is that it helps the development of the basics – those scales of training – without the hindrance of the weight of the rider. The horse can learn to go in the circle with rhythm, suppleness, connection, producing impulsion, being straight and ultimately collected.

A fourth major benefit is that it is an excellent means of allowing the horse to get rid of his high spirits without bucking off the rider or running away. It is a way of avoiding the dangers of getting into a battle to establish control.

THE TACK

The tack needed for lungeing will vary according to the horse and the circumstances. In all cases, the horse is best lunged in a cavesson with a lunge line of at least twenty metres in length and with a lungeing whip that is long enough to reach the horse without the lunger having to go towards him. He should wear brushing boots or bandages, and if the horse is exuberant and might hit his forefeet, it is wise to use overreach boots. In most cases, except for when the mouth has been damaged, it is advisable to wear a snaffle bridle, but this is best used without any noseband in order to avoid pinching under the cavesson. As the lungeing progresses and the horse accepts the work with obedience and calmness, then a roller and side reins can be introduced.

THE METHOD

When lungeing, think of the lunge line as corresponding to the reins in the hands, and the lunge whip to the legs and the seat. Just as in riding, it is important to keep a soft elastic contact through the lunge rein. If the contact is dropped and then re-established with a jerk, it is very difficult for the horse to keep his balance. The trainer should try to stand opposite the horse's girth and try to establish a triangle with the rein acting as one side, the whip the other, and the horse the third, the short side of the triangle.

It is difficult for lungeing to achieve its objectives if

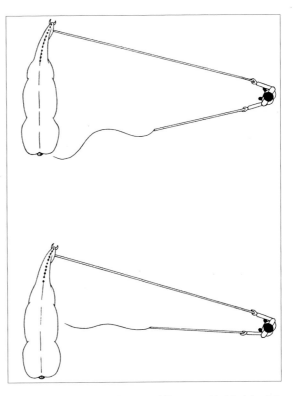

The use of the whip in lungeing. When used behind (top) it helps to encourage him to go forwards and develop more impulsion. Used where the girth would be (below) it helps to keep him out on the circle

it is done on the side of a hill, on bad going, or in an open space where the horse may easily get distracted. Try to find an area where the horse can be lunged in a circle of 20 metres in diameter. It should be flat, as it is very difficult for a horse to balance himself on a slope, and particularly a young horse. Ideally the surface should be artificial and secure (like sand) so the horse does not slip, as this will cause him to lose his confidence and become tense. If the surface is soft it will also help him to develop those springy elastic strides needed in dressage. In order to keep his attention it is best to lunge him in an enclosed space; if this is not available, choose a corner of a field, and the other two sides can be blocked off with, for example, poles and uprights used for show jumping.

Ideally, the trainer should be able to pivot around one point so that the horse is working on a true circle, but in practice this is usually only possible with trained horses. The primary aim is to maintain contact at all times through the lunge rein, and to achieve this it is often necessary to walk in quite large circles. Also it may be necessary for the trainer to come forward a little and to use his whip pointed towards the shoulder if the horse starts to fall in on the circle; or he may have to fall back level with the hindquarters if it is necessary to drive the horse more forward. When teaching the horse to lunge, it gives the trainer more control if he adopts this driving position, and has a relatively short lunge rein so that he walks quite a large circle. Some people like to use an assistant in these early stages of lungeing, who can lead the horse and guide him onto the circle leaving the trainer as the pivot in the centre.

Lungeing is strenuous exercise for the young horse and it is best to concentrate on the walk and trot for quite a number of sessions. Only when calm and relaxed at the trot and the trainer feels the horse is ready to try the canter, then keep him on a large circle and ask him to canter but for only a few strides. It is also important to work equally on both sides, so aim to change the rein frequently.

THE AIMS

The aims when lungeing are the same as those when riding, *ie* the basics, the 'scales' of training. The first requirement is to get the horse going forward in a rhythm; this can be done either at the walk or the trot. The horse must also let go and rid himself of tension. If he is a very high-spirited animal, it is probably best to let him trot around at first. It is a mistake to try and make him walk when it is difficult to make him do so, as he will soon realise that he can avoid obeying the trainer and may lose respect for him.

With the high-spirited horse the trainer can use a soothing voice to settle him into a rhythm. If on the other hand the horse is lazy, then respect needs to be gained as soon as possible and it might be necessary to use the lunge whip on the quarters or just above the hocks to make him realise that he is meant to go forward and use himself energetically.

THE VOICE

The voice is an important aid in lungeing. The horse understands not so much the actual word used, but the tone with which that word is spoken. To ask the horse to slow down, use deep tones and speak very slowly. This request can be reinforced with gentle tugs on the lunge rein. To ask the horse to increase his activity, to trot on or canter, use a sharper, shriller voice and reinforce this with, if necessary, a little crack of the whip or a tap on his hindquarters or just above his hock.

If the horse tends to rush off, then it is easier to settle him in a relatively small circle. Talk to him in soothing tones and frequently ask him to stop, pat him, and start again. This should only be used in the last resort and for a short time. If the horse develops the habit of suddenly taking hold of the outside rein and trying to get away from the circle, use side reins and with the inside rein two or three holes shorter. In this case the lunger's reactions need to be very quick and he should keep a little further behind, opposite the hindquarters rather than where the saddle would be. Great emphasis must be placed on maintaining a soft elastic contact through the lunge rein – never allow the horse the opportunity to loosen it, then snatch at it, to dash off to the outside. Keep varying the pressure very slightly so that he knows you have control.

PROBLEMS

Lungeing does take experience and if problems arise, seek expert advice. The following are suggestions for correcting some of the simpler problems. It was suggested above that if the horse falls in on the circle, the whip could be pointed at his shoulder; if this is not effective, then before taking the horse out to the lungeing area, place some blocks or buckets in a circle of a diameter of about twelve to fifteen metres. The horse can then be lunged so that he goes round the outside of these and will necessarily be kept out.

Another common problem is the horse that will not stop. Select a very tall hedge or side of the school which he will not jump, then ask him to halt using the voice and checks with the lunge rein. If this is not successful then move yourself and direct him towards the tall hedge or wall, asking him to stop at the same time. He will be forced to do so. Pat and reward him. Start again, ask him to halt; if he does not do so, head him again towards the obstacle until he learns what is required.

SIDE REINS

When the horse goes on a circle on both reins with rhythm and suppleness, using his muscles along his back and top line, then the side reins can be introduced (usually after about half-a-dozen sessions on the lunge). These are attached between the roller and the bit, and in the first instance are pretty loose. The horse is then lunged in them and driven forward, without allowing him to run, until he accepts the contact. If the side reins are so long that the horse cannot establish a contact, then they can be progressively shortened, but never beyond a point that they bring the horse's face behind the vertical.

It is not advisable ever to lead a horse in side reins or to allow him to walk on the lunge with them on for more than a dozen strides. It is always best to start a lungeing session without side reins, and to remove them again at the end of the session when he finishes with a trot, stretching his head and neck forward and down.

When the horse is young, most of the work on the lunge is done at the trot. However, the lunge is a very useful means of getting the horse to establish a balance in the canter and to learn to strike off smoothly. Therefore when the horse is starting to be ridden away in canter in the open, he can be lunged for short periods at this same pace; it helps to make frequent transitions between the trot and canter. However, only after he has established a good balance and is taking springy strides in a clear three beat, should he be cantered for more than two or three circuits.

If it is obvious that the horse is on the wrong bend on the lunge, then the inside side rein can be shortened by one or possibly two holds. As soon as the wrong bend has been corrected, then return to side reins of equal length.

Many trainers do not use side reins at all. Personally I feel it does depend upon the horse. If the horse tends to come behind the bit it takes great skill to be able to drive him forward to establish a true contact on side reins. In this particular

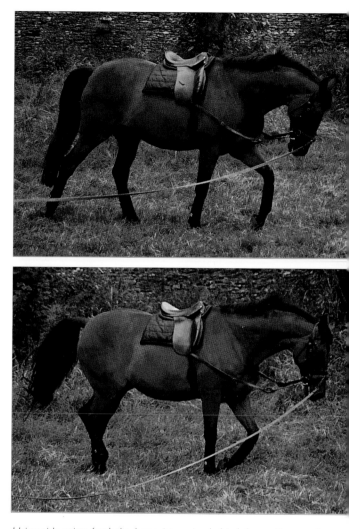

Using side reins: (top) the horse is coming behind the vertical and (below) the horse is falling onto his forehand and not making a contact

case it is all too easy to make the situation even worse by using side reins, and it might be advisable to allow such a horse to work in freedom.

OTHER EXERCISES

It is a useful exercise on the lunge to trot over poles. These can either be scattered around singly and the horse occasionally asked to trot over one at a time, or as he progresses in his training to arrange them on the circle at regular intervals. These are discussed in more detail below. As the aim of dressage is to make the horse as gymnastic as possible, it can also help to jump him over small fences on the lunge. The side reins must be removed for this. I use very small fences, either a cross pole or simply a pole with its outside end on a block and its inside end – towards the lunger – on the ground. It teaches the horse to be neat and nimble as he manoeuvres himself over these small fences. The trainer, however, has to be skilful and give him the best possible chance of tackling them with ease. He should give him two or three straight strides into any trotting pole or jump and he should not ask the horse to attempt one until he is trotting or cantering in an easy, balanced rhythm.

Later on, lungeing can also be used to develop some lengthened strides at the trot. This can be achieved by gradually bringing him into a smaller circle, which will help him to step actively underneath with his hind legs and then allowing him out onto a larger circle and encouraging him to go forward. If he starts to run then he should be steadied into a working trot again.

Lungeing is a wonderful aid to training if it is done with thought and care. The best lungers are usually also the best riders as lungeing entails feeling and anticipating what the horse is about to do, and correcting it, if need be, before it actually happens. Good lungeing also entails the use of discipline without making the horse sour and fed up. It is as important to reward the horse when he is good – with the voice, and when he is standing, by giving him a pat and possibly a titbit – as

it is to know when the horse is being obstinate and needs a reprimand or stronger demands, or when he has done enough and is getting tired.

POLES

Poles are a very useful aid to dressage training. They can be placed on the ground or on blocks between four and six inches high, and can be used in the warming up of a horse as they help the loosening up. They also provide variety, giving the horse an interesting new approach to his work. Most important, however, they encourage him to flex his joints and to swing through his back. To achieve this, if being ridden over them the rider must be soft in his back as any stiffness will be relayed to the horse and will hinder this beneficial effect of pole work.

Another benefit of pole work is to help in the lengthening and shortening of strides. Horses with bold and free walks often have difficulty in collecting, but by progressively shortening the distance between the poles, the horse can be encouraged to do so. Vice versa, a horse with rather a short walk that does not naturally overtrack can be encouraged to lengthen his stride by progressively lengthening the distance between the poles. These same objectives can be pursued at the trot to help lengthening and/or collecting.

When using the poles, it is crucial that the distances suit the horse. Those that are given below

Trotting over poles and showing how it encourages the horse to lift his legs and flex his joints

Walking over poles and showing how this encourages the horse to stretch forward and down, to round his neck and back

are average distances, but as a major purpose of the exercise is to get the horse relaxed and swinging 'through', it is important not to make him tense because he is finding it difficult to take the length of the stride set. An assistant on the ground can adjust distances, especially in the early stages before the trainer knows the length of his horse's strides.

The other important factors are to approach the poles on both reins equally; and when going over the poles, to allow the horse to stretch forward and down – but not so far that he falls onto his forehand.

To start off with, just use one pole, then two, and three; four is the normal maximum. At the walk the distance between the poles should be just under the metre, and at the trot over the metre. At first the poles should be on the ground but later they can be raised and put on the blocks. If used at the canter, they should always be on blocks and a minimum of about .5m high. The distance between them then is about 3.5m, and it is best for the rider to tackle these poles in a forward seat.

On the lunge, the poles can be arranged on the circumference of a circle – the distance between them will be shorter towards the centre of the circle, longer on the outside, and should be at the optimum in the centre.

If there is space available, it helps the warming-up to have poles to walk over, and three or four poles set at the walk distance can be left perma-

nently on the ground; the horse tends to look at them, and thus lowers his head stretching it forward and down, lengthening the back muscles; this helps him to loosen up.

GYMNASTIC JUMPING

Gymnastic jumping is another excellent aid for training the dressage horse. Like the poles, it provides variety and as a more exciting type of exercise, helps to freshen up the horse. It also has useful physical benefits, for in gymnastic jumping the aim is to get the horse to use his back over the fences (to

Jumping is good for the dressage rider, getting him to think forward and follow the horse's movement over the fence, and good for the horse to make him more impulsive and gymnastic

bascule), and this will have beneficial effects on the work on the flat. It also tends to help a lazy horse, or a horse that is a little behind the bit, to take more positive contact and develop more impulsion.

To start with, gymnastic jumping is an extension of pole work. Place two or three trotting poles at a distance of about 1.45m (depending on the length of stride of the horse) with the last about 2.9m away from a very small crossbar. When the horse jumps this calmly and in a good rhythm, then another fence can be placed 5.8m away from the crossbar. Keep it very small, but it will have the greatest gymnastic effect if this second fence is a small parallel.

The objective of these exercises is not to turn the horse into a show jumper but to improve his dressage. The fences can be kept low to build up his confidence, to keep him calm and relaxed so it helps

to make him more supple and develop his impulsion. The sessions should be short so he enjoys them and does not get too tired.

There are many variations on this basic approach. The trotting poles can be taken away and just one placing pole left. It is usually advisable to keep the crossbar as a nice easy introduction and to use the second fence for variations – for example, it can be raised or widened, or the distance to it can be varied depending on the horse. If he needs to be taught to compress himself, to engage the hindquarters, the distance can be reduced; if he needs to be encouraged to go forward more, to lengthen his stride, the distance can be increased. The important factor is to make these changes in distance progressive.

It is vital in this work always to have an assistant available, not just to put up the fences, but to check and alter the distances as necessary so they suit the horse and enable him to jump calmly and with rhythm.

Experienced jumping riders can introduce a great variety of gymnastic exercises to help improve the horse's work on the flat. Most dressage riders, however, do not do a great deal of jumping, and for them this simple format will be sufficient to give their horse some variety and help him to use his back.

LOOSE SCHOOLING

For those fortunate enough to have an indoor school, or an artificial arena surrounded with a high fence, or even a loose schooling lane, then allowing the horse to go free around this area is another useful exercise in the training. The ideal area is about 20 × 30m. It can be smaller than this, but if larger then more assistants will be needed and more poles to guide the horse around the outside of the school. To help him to do this, place blocks about 8m in from each corner and poles on either side of them, so that he is clearly directed around the outside track.

Bouncing in and out of cross poles helps to make the horse more gymnastic

In the first lesson, three people should be available to help show him the way. One is positioned in the middle and one at either end, and all three have small whips. When the horse first comes into the area and is let loose, it is best to just let him go round free to accustom himself to the area, and to let off any high spirits with a good buck and a canter. He should wear a headcollar and protective boots. As soon as he has settled, then direct him around the outside track, using the voice to encourage him to trot. When he settles into a rhythm on one rein, then guide him across the diagonal by standing in front of him as he comes along the track of one of the long sides, and direct him so he changes the rein and trots around the other way. When he does this calmly, ask him to halt with the same voice used when lungeing, and reward him with pats, and possibly a titbit.

The aim in these early stages is to get the horse to go round in a relaxed, rhythmical manner. If he does this in the first lesson then that is sufficient; in further lessons there are a number of alternative exercises. A roller and side reins can be put on after he has loosened up and is going round in a good, swinging, rhythmical trot. These should be attached at the same length as when lungeing, so there is a contact but without restricting him so much that his head comes behind the vertical. He can then be asked to steady around the short side and to lengthen his strides down the long side. Never use side reins if jumping the horse.

Loose jumping is fun for the young horse and also stimulating. He should wear overreach boots and no side reins. Start by putting the odd pole down on the ground along the long side. Even if it is only a pole on the ground, place wings at the side so that he never gets into the habit of running out. When he goes over these poles quite happily, then one of the poles on the ground can be used as a placing pole 2.9m away from a very small crossbar. This crossbar should have wings, and a pole running from the upright on the inside down onto the ground, to guide him towards the fence. When he jumps this well, then put the placing pole the other side and direct him so he jumps it on the other rein. The crossbar can then be raised and/or a pole put

behind it so it becomes a small spread, or if there is room, another fence placed 5.8m away from it. As in gymnastic jumping exercises, these distances will need to be shortened or lengthened according to the horse and the going in the school — if it is very deep then the horse will need shorter distances.

It is important to make the loose schooling a fun exercise for the horse, not to frighten him by putting up big fences or allowing him to rush at them. If he does start to rush, revert to the easier exercises ie just poles on the ground, and stop him frequently to pat him and reward him with titbits. One person should be in charge of the operation and tell the assistants what to do to ensure the horse tackles the fences at the best possible speed.

LONG REINING

Long reining is another form of training associated with dressage. It is, however, very difficult to do well, and is rarely to the horse's benefit unless the person who does the long reining is very experienced, has spent many years riding and is therefore able to anticipate a horse's moves and able to feel in his hands what the horse is doing and about to do. It is a skill best learnt by working with the top exponents and is not therefore within the scope of this book on practical dressage.

ARENA WORK

Arena work is where the serious dressage training is done. Obviously it is best if such training can be done in an indoor school or an outdoor school with an artificial surface. As has been emphasised earlier, it is important for a dressage horse to work on a secure surface and one that does not jar him. Grass can provide a very good surface, especially old turf, but the problem is that with the variations in the weather the trainer will have to be careful when it is very hard, wet or deep. If working in a field it is best to mark out an arena 20 x 40m, or 20 x 60m, to get a horse used to working in that area. Barrels or blocks can be used to mark the corners and it is useful also to put one at the middle of each long side, at B and E. Obviously the more the arena can be enclosed the easier it is to keep the horse's attention but these six blocks are sufficient. Buckets can be used for dressage markers; they are easily painted with the letters A, C, H, K, and so on, and can then be put at the appropriate points to help the test riding.

With a grass arena it is best to move the site slightly quite often so that the track does not become marked and hard or uneven for the horse to work on.

LOOSENING UP

Arena work begins with a loosening up session. Most dressage horses will have been in the stable for the previous twenty-three hours, and need time to unstiffen and settle to the new environment. Different riders have different approaches. Some take them for a walk, some go into the arena and walk them around on a free rein. Some start straightaway with pretty collected work in the walk *ie* shoulder in, half passes and such like. Others take the horse over those poles set at the walk distance. Personally I prefer to give the horse an undemanding time until he has really let go his muscles and established his balance.

Use rising trot – if he tends to pull, keep on a circle to settle him rather than starting a fight with the reins. If he is lazy, try to keep to straight lines and shallow curves. When starting to canter it is often helpful to use the forward seat as this keeps the weight off the back and allows him to stretch those important muscles and start them working. If, however, the horse tends to canter croup high, or to pull down onto his forehand, it may be necessary to canter in the basic position, but with as little weight as possible in the saddle. Try to put the weight down into the stirrups rather than on the seat bones.

The aim of this loosening up is to allow the horse physically to let go his muscles so that he is prepared in the best possible way for the work ahead, and that mentally he is calm enough to accept the aids from the rider. This means that the length of the loosening up sessions will vary considerably for different horses. The high-spirited, temperamental horse may take quite a time to settle into a rhythm and to relax. So also might the stiff horse, and for very young horses this loosening up period will be the majority of the arena work.

Loosening up by cantering in a forward seat so as not to restrict the horse's back. The rider is encouraging this horse to round up and become more supple

In the loosening up work it does not matter so much if the horse comes a little behind the vertical as long as he is working forwards to the bit

When the horse is going with rhythm and suppleness so that if the rider releases the reins he will champ the reins out of the rider's hands, then he is ready for the work session, the second stage of arena work.

THE WORK SESSION

The primary objective remains the establishment of the basics, those scales of training – rhythm, suppleness, connection, impulsion, straightness and ultimately collection. At first these are worked on directly, but progressively movements are introduced which, apart from being an end in themselves, also help to further develop the basics. There will be plenty of occasions during the training when the basics are lost, especially

In the work session the horse is asked to engage more so that he can lighten and raise his shoulders, neck and head. He then becomes more manoeuvreable and able to do the movements

when trying to make the horse understand a particular movement, or in overcoming his resistance to a novel concept. The important factor is that the horse is made to understand what is required of him, and that the basics are then re-established as quickly as possible by returning to simpler work.

For instance, when simply turning a sharper corner or riding a smaller circle, the horse might lose his rhythm. He should be asked to complete that smaller circle, but then return to a larger circle to re-establish the rhythm; however, keep returning to ask for the smaller circle until he can complete it with rhythm – this may be done in one day or it may need two weeks, or more.

Another important factor is never to exhaust the horse during this work session. With the young horse who is only just getting used to the weight of the rider it is particularly important that he enjoys the work. If he is forced to do it when he tired and exhausted, he will soon become reluctant to do it at all.

To help the horse from getting tired too quickly, and for his muscles to retain tone without becoming stiffened through exhaustion, it is helpful to give the horse short breaks during this second stage of the arena work. Some riders like to return to the walk and go on a free rein. Others allow the horse to champ the reins out of the hands either at the canter or the trot. Whatever exercise is used, it is important that the horse is not allowed to fall onto the forehand. It is simply an opportunity for him to stretch his muscles, which if he has been working correctly he will want to do, and the activity of the hindquarters should be retained so that he rounds his back and stretches forward and down.

These breaks should only be for a short time, then return to whatever work is planned for that day – this will depend on the stage of training (refer to the chart on p108 to check what is appropriate). It is important that the training plan incorporates plenty of variety each day. However, in no one work session can all the movements be tackled. Plan one or two projects each day and vary them so that different ones are tackled on the next day, or the day after.

With a horse, however, all good plans must be adjustable. If he comes out in a cantankerous frame of mind, the plan to progress the training may well have to be abandoned in the interests of re-establishing the basics. If, on the other hand, he comes out in a co-operative mood and physically in a good state, then seize the opportunity to progress the training a little more than anticipated.

The important factors are to give variety to his work and not to tire him so much that it becomes a great labour. One of the major aims of dressage is getting the horse to work 'with' you, not 'for' you.

At the end of the work session the horse is rewarded with pats and allowed to stretch forwards and down

This does not mean spoiling him; he must respect his rider and learn to try his hardest. This will entail the occasional reprimand and demand to 'try harder', but when he does so there must also be the reward.

COOLING OFF

The work sessions should be aimed at progressing the training, getting him to engage further, to complete a slightly tighter circle, etc. This will put demands on him both mentally and physically, and he should relax again before returning to his stable. The third stage of the arena work is the cooling off and relaxing session. Many trainers just go on a walk on a free rein, or even hand their horse over to somebody else to lead around or ride out. Others allow the horse to champ the reins out of the fingers, but this is a much abused and misunderstood exercise. It is only of benefit if it is done well and does not mean that all the contact is lost when he tends to fall onto his forehand, and even slightly hollow the top line. The aims are that he continues in the same rhythm with the same engagement of hindquarters, but gradually stretches his frame which he rounds in a similar fashion to a horse that does a good bascule over a fence. The rider should retain the contact with the legs to encourage the continuing engagement and maintenance of rhythm but gradually ease the pressure in his fingers to allow the horse to take the reins forward and down. The horse should not be allowed to snatch the reins, nor to lunge forward onto the forehand, nor to change his rhythm. This exercise can be done in the canter or the trot. At the walk the walk on a free rein is based on the same principles. At the end of the session the horse can do this stretching down on both reins and is then walked to dry off. If there is time give him a walk across a field or down the road to keep him fresh. Some trainers like to return their horses to the yard quickly if they are hot, give them a wash down and then cool them off when they are led around or walked out with the rider in the saddle. The important factor is that the horse goes back to his stable cool and relaxed.

One of the best features about dressage is that the preparation is fun. The training every day is always full of challenges, a never-ending series of problems that need tackling, and the prospect of that wonderful elation when they are solved or at least progress made.

EQUIPMENT FOR THE TRAINING

BITS In everyday training the essential items are the saddle, bridle, numnah, boots or bandages. Most dressage riders like to use a snaffle bit with loose rings; the mouthpiece is quite thick and light and jointed in the middle and it is commonly referred to as the German snaffle. The majority of dressage horses work in this snaffle until they change to the double and many riders still continue to ride them in it at home. It is the bit in which it is easiest to establish that elastic, consistent contact with most horses.

There are, however, horses that are reluctant to take hold of a bit so the contact feels very light and inconsistent; in this case it is best to use a heavier mouthpiece and fixed rings. The Fulmer snaffle is one of the most useful types for getting a horse to take a stronger contact. Other options are a rubber snaffle or the various types of synthetic snaffles now on the market. For the horse that takes too strong a contact then the French bridoon with the two links in the middle is often the answer. Some horses will respond better to a thinner mouthpiece but this should only be a short term correction. The aim must be to return to a broader, milder mouthpiece as this is the best way of achieving a true contact.

NOSEBANDS Dressage riders use three types of noseband. The cavesson is the mildest, but many prefer the drop or flash noseband which helps to ensure that the horse does not develop any bad habits like opening his mouth or putting his tongue out. It is important, however, that neither of these two versions of the noseband are done up so tightly that the horse feels restricted as this will only develop more resistance. It should be possible to put two fingers between the noseband and the horse's skin, so that he has a little freedom but will feel the restriction if he starts to resist.

THE SADDLE is a crucial part of the equipment. A good one can help the rider to establish his position; a bad one can make it very difficult for him to do so. If good, it can make the horse comfortable and happy to work through his back; if bad it may unbalance him, make him sore and reluctant to work, and make him hollow his back rather than rounding and softening it.

The saddle must fit the rider. The seat is better to be too big than too short. If too short, the rider will find it difficult to sit on the flat area, and will either be perched up the pommel or on the cantle, both of which are unbalancing. The flaps must be long enough so that the rider's boots do not get caught on the edge and far enough forward for the knee to rest comfortably. It is a matter of choice what type of seat the rider chooses, whether it is the deep seat which encourages him to sit in one position and makes it difficult for him to move, or the flatter seat which gives him much more freedom to move but less support to stay in a position. The classical schools, the Spanish Riding School and Oliviera in Portugal, use the flatter seats, and it seems that more and more of today's riders are turning to this type.

The saddle must fit the horse; without a numnah it should sit on his back and there should be no air between it and the horse, either at the front where it rests on the upper part of the shoulder, or on the back where it rests in front of the loins. It must not touch his spine so it is wise to choose a saddle with a broad and reasonably high channel through it. The pommel too must be high enough to clear the withers. The horse tends to be more comfortable if the weight of the rider is spread evenly over a larger area, *ie* with the flatter seated saddles. Beware of panels which are slightly concave and rounded as this leads to a rocking effect on the horse, producing friction and soreness.

A numnah is used under the saddle. There are many varieties, some riders favouring sheepskins, others just plain cottons, others the various synthetic fabrics. The crucial factor is that any numnah is kept very clean and frequently washed in an anti-allergy powder, and very carefully rinsed clean of any soap.

8

Problems and Corrections

The best way to approach dressage is to establish clear goals and work systematically towards them. It is part of the dressage scene however that judges, trainers and experienced onlookers will point out weaknesses in the work. In the following pages some of the most common criticisms are listed, their meaning discussed and some suggestions made as to how they might be remedied. Remember that this list is far from comprehensive, as for each problem there are usually numerous possible causes and even more remedies.

Remember too when working on a single problem to keep the whole picture, and the goals, in mind. It is easy to get sidetracked and lose some of your good work if you focus too much on remedying the faults.

There is no doubt that this is horse is on his forehand. With his weight distributed in such a way it would be difficult for him to do the dressage movements

ON THE FOREHAND/LACKING ENGAGEMENT

PROBLEM

The weight is carried mainly by the forehand with the hind legs being behind rather than under the horse.

POSSIBLE CAUSES AND REMEDIES

When the horse falls onto his forehand and lacks engagement, he is also likely to lose his balance and rhythm (see below). Dressage training is geared to transferring the weight backwards off the forehand so the horse carries more of it on his hindlegs. Although transitions and half halts are probably the most directly effective means of getting a horse off his forehand, all the movements ie circles, shoulder in, half passes – if done well – should help to transfer the weight backwards so he becomes more engaged. The rider can also help by ensuring that his own weight distribution is directly

This pony is on his forehand; his hindquarters are not engaged, but the rider is doing well to retain an upright position

The rider is tipping forward as the horse falls onto his forehand, and this will mean there is even more weight on the shoulders

A horse in a good shoulder in, which is encouraging him to engage and lighten his forehand

above the horse's centre of gravity. Many riders tend to lean forward and put more weight onto the horse's shoulders, particularly in rising trot and sometimes at the canter. It is important to keep the weight directly above the seat bones and remain in an upright position if the rider is to help the horse keep the weight off the forehand.

LOSS OF BALANCE/RHYTHM

PROBLEM

The horse loses his balance to change the speed of the rhythm (tempo) of the work. He will usually move his head to try and help rebalance himself, either putting it up in the air or leaning on the rider's hands.

POSSIBLE CAUSES AND REMEDIES

1 Untrained horse, finding it difficult to accommodate the weight of the rider – more training and strengthening of muscles.
2 Unbalanced rider, sitting to one side or moving unnecessarily – rider to work on position.
3 Falling onto forehand – this will be hard to prevent in the young horse but training should be done, with half halts and transitions between and within paces, to help the horse engage his hindquarters.
4 Falling onto shoulder with the horse losing his uprightness. He leans to one side to put more weight on one foreleg and shoulder than the other. This occurs when he is not straight and is aggravated if the rider asks for too much bend in the neck, with the horse bending from the wither and therefore pushing weight onto the outside shoulder – use shoulder fore and shoulder in (pp97–8); ride in circles to the direction in which he puts too much weight on the shoulder, with the rider asking for a distinct bend round the inside leg; and in circles on the rein to which he bends too much, with more positive use of the outside rein, use counter flexion bending him to the outside (see fig left).

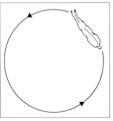

5 Hurrying; the horse starts to run rather then swing 'through' in a clear rhythm – slow down with half halts, engage the hindquarters more, and keep the horse calm.

A horse showing the tension and lack of submission that are so often the result of a loss of balance and rhythm

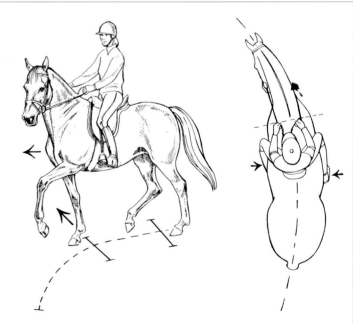

The strong use of the inside rein and big bend in the neck has resulted in the weight falling onto the outside shoulder, making it difficult for the horse to obey the aids and turn

The goal – a well-balanced turn

ABOVE THE BIT

PROBLEM

The horse resists the rider by stiffening at the poll, in the neck, and usually in the back, to carry his head high.

This young rider has lost the contact and the pony is stiffening his neck and coming above the bit

POSSIBLE CAUSES AND REMEDIES

1 Lack of basics – the most common cause is lack of training. The horse does not go in a rhythm and with balance, is not sufficiently supple and is difficult to connect. Work on the basic and the horse will automatically come onto the bit.

2 Discomfort – the horse is likely to go above the bit if he has a sore mouth, if his teeth are rough and sharp, or if he has a back problem and tries to hollow away from the rider's weight. Check and correct these problems as necessary.

3 The rider can cause the horse to go above the bit if he has a bad seat, making it uncomfortable for the horse to carry him – he may try to avoid doing so by hollowing his back and lifting his head into the air. If the rider has rough hands

and tries to pull back, many horses object by going against the contact and putting their heads in the air. Such a rider must work on his position.

4 Resistance and obstinate nature – the rider will have to make it clear to the horse that he wants him to go work on the bit. He will have to make the horse understand his aids and persuade him to obey them. This is achieved by not pulling on the reins to lower the head, as although in the short term this might have a result, in the long term the horse will resist. Also, pulling on the reins tends to send the hindlegs further out behind, so making it genuinely more difficult for the horse to come on the bit. The answer is to ask him to go forward with the leg aids into the rider's hands. If a horse tends to stiffen and hollow, then the rider can maintain a non-allowing contact until he feels the horse soften, when he should yield the reins slightly. As soon as the horse starts to resist and go above the bit again, then the rider establishes that non-allowing, more positive contact with the hands and rides up to the hands with the leg aids, and the seat if the horse does not hollow against it. The crucial factor is to recognise when the horse is about to accept and to yield the pressure in the reins

so that the horse feels comfortable when he is on the bit.

An exercise which can help to get difficult horses on the bit is to walk in small circles, asking for a positive bend to the inside, using plenty of inside leg. As soon as the horse accepts the inside aids then the rider should relax the contact a little, and allow the horse to balance on the outside rein. As soon as he feels soft in this position ride him forward into the trot. If he starts to resist, return to work on the small circle at the walk, and go through the same process.

Another useful exercise (see *figure below*) is to spiral into a smaller circle in a working trot, and then to ask the horse to step sideways in leg yield out into the larger circle on which he was originally trotting. The crucial factor is to leg yield with

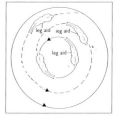

only a slight flexion and use the inside leg to little checks in the outside rein. The feeling in the inside rein should be soft and the rider should not have to pull on it to keep the bend.

This young horse has tightened his muscles and is just starting to come above the bit. This could be a nervous reaction to the new, strange experience of competition

BEHIND THE BIT

A horse that has come well behind the vertical, and it appears as if the rider has a pretty strong contact on the inside rein which can aggravate this problem

This horse has also come behind the vertical, but not nearly so severely as in the above photograph, and the white froth indicates he is taking an elastic contact with the bit

PROBLEM

The horse drops his head behind the vertical to try and avoid taking the contact with the hands of the rider through the reins. In training there are likely to be occasions when the horse's head does come behind the vertical, but as long as he is still taking a positive elastic contact and is ready to go forward as required, this is rarely a problem. It is only when he brings his head behind the vertical to try and avoid the contact, as a form of resistance, that corrections are needed.

POSSIBLE CAUSES AND REMEDIES

1 Discomfort – as in 'Above the bit' (p129).
2 Rider – pulls on the rein, is rough with his hands and encourages the horse to avoid the contact. It is strong use of the inside rein that is one of the most common causes of overbending. The rider must work on achieving a more balanced position, quieter hands and to keep easing the pressure on the inside rein.
3 Obstinacy and/or resistance – the rider should take a positive contact but with a forward feeling (no tendency to pull) in his hands and ride the horse positively forward into this contact. As soon as the horse takes a slightly stronger feel, then he can lighten the hands, particularly the inside rein if he is on a circle, to encourage the horse to take his head further forward.

It is very important that the rider keeps still, steady hands with horses that have this problem. The tendency to move the hands will provoke the horse into a further resistance and bring his head even further into his chest to avoid the contact.
4 Too sharp a bit – try milder snaffle.

HEAD UNSTEADY/NODDING

PROBLEM

The horse moves his head either from side to side or up and down.

POSSIBLE CAUSES AND REMEDIES

1 Hard hands – the rider moves his hands and the horse has no confidence in the contact and tries to avoid it. Some riders use a see-saw action with the hands to get the head into the correct position. The rider must work on achieving a better position, and establishing a soft, steady contact through the reins.

2 Lack of impulsion – particularly in the canter, the head will nod up and down if the horse lacks engagement and is not going forwards. See 'Lacking impulsion', p133.

3 Resistance – the horse moves his head to try and avoid taking the contact with the rider's hands. The rider should take a positive but soft feel with the reins and ride forward into the hands using the leg and seat aids.

4 Discomfort – see p133.

TILTING

PROBLEM

The horse tilts and holds his head at an angle ie when turning on a circle to the right, the jaw is further in than the poll.

POSSIBLE CAUSES AND REMEDIES

1 Physical problem – if the horse has a neck or back injury he might tilt his head. Check with a vet or specialist in this field.

2 The rider is trying to pull him around the corner using a strong inside rein – the horse should be ridden more positively into the outside rein with the rider using the inside leg and little checks on the outside rein at the same time as easing the contact on the inside rein.

3 Horse unbalanced and tilts his head to keep upright – work on balancing and straightening the horse and check rider's position is upright, and the weight correctly distributed as this is often the cause of the problem.

The tilt of the head to the left is distinctly clear in this photograph

WRONG BEND

PROBLEM

When the horse goes round a corner his flexion is to the outside rather than to the inside.

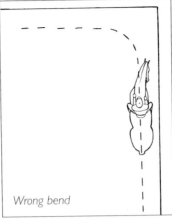
Wrong bend

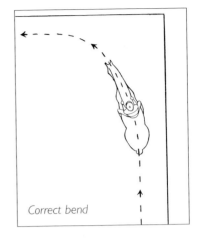
Correct bend

This novice rider is using the outside rein to keep her pony on the track, and he is bending to the outside

Right: This rider is positioned to take his horse off to the left as his shoulders and body are turned in that direction. In fact the horse is turning right, but he has to do so in a wrong bend

POSSIBLE CAUSES AND REMEDIES

1 Riding too far into the corners – the rider is asking the horse to go further into the corners than he is capable of at the stage of training, and is therefore having to use the outside rein to pull him onto this tight track. Make the turns smoother and more shallow.

2 Rider's aids – these are incorrect; either he is trying to keep the horse out on the required track of the circle by pulling with the outside rein, or he is not in a balanced position round the turn himself *ie* he is not turning his shoulders with those of the horse, but is turning towards the outside which will encourage the horse to go in the wrong bend. The horse must learn to turn with a uniform bend to the line of the corner around the rider's inside leg. The rider must be able to use his inside leg with gentle supportive nudges, and the horse must learn to respond to this. Leg yielding (p96) and shoulder fore (p97) can help him to become more responsive to an inside leg and to learn to step into the contact of the outside rein rather than falling into a wrong bend. As the horse progresses, shoulder in (p98) is an even more useful exercise to establish this.

LACKING IMPULSION

PROBLEM

Impulsion is the power of the horse; it is the energy created in the hindquarters which is transmitted 'through' a swinging back into a soft elastic contact in the hands. The criticism 'lack of impulsion' is probably made more often than any other on a judge's sheet, as impulsion is very difficult to develop and control. Then there is the danger that those that try to aim for a great deal of impulsion frequently make their horses tense and uncontrollable. With a high-spirited horse, a lack of impulsion might even be beneficial in the early stages to help keep him calm and in balance.

POSSIBLE CAUSES AND REMEDIES

1 Lack of desire to go forward – the horse may be bored and unresponsive. His work should become more varied, he can be taken on canters, with another horse to encourage him to want to go forward more. It may also be due to weakness or to laziness, and in the latter he should be made more responsive to the aids, reinforcing a leg aid with taps of the stick and use of spurs. Remember, however, that the horse soon becomes dulled to these additional aids if they are used in the rhythm of the strides and/or too frequently.
2 Lack of engagement – the source of impulsion is the engagement of the hindquarters; if they are not engaged, it may be due to a lack of muscular development, or to conformation, or to poor training which has not asked the horse for sufficient engagement. If the latter, then half halts and transitions within and between paces are most helpful.
3 Stiffening – impulsion will not be contained within the horse if, when being transmitted through the back and neck to the reins, it meets any resistance. Any stiffening of the back, neck or mouth will mean a loss of impulsion, and work must be done to ensure the horse becomes more supple.

4 Lack of straightness – if the horse is not straight then the energy developed in the hind legs will not be able to go through to the hands but will be directed out through a shoulder. Work must be done on making the horse straighter (see 'Not Straight', p135).

This pony looks pretty submissive but the steps are likely to be rather flat with no suspension. It is time to create more impulsion

NOT WORKING 'THROUGH'

PROBLEM

The horse works 'through' when his quarters, back, neck, poll and mouth are linked ie there is no resistance to the energy created in the hindquarters being transmitted 'through' the body into the hands.

POSSIBLE CAUSES AND REMEDIES

1 Rider – the rider does not ask his horse to work from behind to the hands, he should initiate all directives with the leg and seat aids rather than the hand aids. Any pulling back will cause resistance and stop the horse working 'through'.
2 Discomfort – any pain in the back or neck will lead to resistance and stop the horse working 'through'. He should be checked, to be sure that this is not the cause, and the fitting of tack examined as this is often a reason.
3 Resistance by the horse – the rider can use various exercises to reduce the resistance, ie circles, shoulder in and so on. He should be sure that he himself asks the horse to go forward into the hands, and that as soon as the horse yields and stops resisting, he allows slightly with his hands.

This is rather an eye-catching combination, but there is an impression of tightness and a rather high neck carriage without the corresponding lightening of the shoulders through engagement of the hindquarters. This lack of true roundness and elasticity of the muscles will make it difficult to work through

NOT STRAIGHT

POSSIBLE CAUSES AND REMEDIES

1 Rider – if the rider does not sit evenly on his seat bones and upright above the horse, then he will tend to affect the straightness of the horse. The rider will have to work on his position.
2 A physical defect – problems in the back or hindlegs can cause the horse not to work straight. Checks should be made to ensure this is not the cause.
3 Natural crookedness – it is very unlikely that a horse will ever become completely straight. Even with good training that corrects a crookedness to one direction, it may often result in the horse becoming slightly crooked to the other direction. To straighten the horse ride him forward. Encourage him to taken even, propulsive steps with his hind legs. Avoid fiddling too much with the reins as this kills the impulsion which is one of the best aids to getting a horse straight. Any rein aids should focus on getting the horse to take a stronger contact on the light side rather than vice versa which is most riders' natural instinct.

The classic exercises to correct straightness are the shoulder fore and shoulder in. Use circles, big ones on the side to which he bends too easily, keeping the horse as straight as possible, and small ones in the direction to which he is reluctant to bend, asking for a positive bend.

To keep a horse straight along the long side of an arena in medium and extended canter is usually quite difficult. The rider should constantly be thinking of positioning his horse in shoulder fore to achieve this. When a horse is not straight, riding him forward into a stronger pace is much more effective than trying to fiddle with the reins. It also helps to ride along the inside track, ie about 1m in from the long side (see Chapter 4).

A horse which is not straight. The hind legs are being carried to the inside, and are not stepping into the same tracks as the corresponding front legs, as they should be on this straight line. The rider is collapsing to the right

LACK OF CADENCE

PROBLEM

The FEI has defined cadence as 'the result of the proper harmony that a horse shows when it moves with well marked regularity, impulsion and balance. The rhythm that a horse maintains in all his paces is an integral part of cadence'. I rather like the simpler one found in some dictionaries of 'a pronounced rhythm'.

POSSIBLE CAUSES AND REMEDIES

All the above – the horse's work will lack cadence, that pronounced rhythm, if he is unbalanced, above the bit, behind the bit, unsteady in the head, tilting, has a wrong bend, lacks impulsion or is not working through. Cadence is an indication that the basics are established and should be maintained in all the different movements including the variations of pace.

A horse showing obvious cadence with clear suspension to the canter and a well-rounded outline

LOSING SELF-CARRIAGE

PROBLEM

A horse is in self carriage when he is in balance, not relying on the reins or stiff muscles to hold him in a position. He should be rounded and with the poll as the highest point, except when he is being worked long and low.

POSSIBLE CAUSES AND REMEDIES

Self carriage is achieved because the hinds are well engaged and the horse is working forwards to a soft elastic contact. When he loses self carriage the rider may need to work on the balance to establish a pronounced tempo to the work, on the suppleness that he is not tightening his muscles or even resisting, on the connection so he is working through to the contact, on the impulsion that he has sufficient power, on the straightness, that he is taking an even contact, and on the collection that he is well engaged with a light forehand. In other words self carriage is the epitome of all the basics.

It should be noted, too, that a horse can achieve these requisites and be in self carriage when he is working long and low as well as when he is in the outline needed for a test.

Top: The poll has dropped and self carriage has been lost

Right: The same horse a little later in the same test, showing good self carriage and proving that many problems can be quickly corrected

9

Preparation for the Competitive Test

The purpose of the dressage test is to test the training of the horse, to assess the quality of the work, how far classical principles have been adhered to, and that the horse's natural ability has been retained or even improved upon. This aspect is much more important than the accuracy with which the test is done on the day. Good judges will recognise this and will reward a good way of going. In any case a horse's training will benefit much more if ridden in the arena with a view to improving his basics, and not to forfeiting them in order to make sure that he halts exactly at X, or does a transition exactly at H. Ultimately, however, the rider wants to achieve both – a good way of going and an accurate test. Nor are they contradictory – when a horse is going well it will be much easier to be accurate.

If the test is not to put back his training, then he will have to be able to do the movements in it with ease. If tackled before the horse is ready for it, the dressage test is likely to result in the basics being forfeited, in him becoming tense and resistant. As a general rule it is best to compete in tests at one level below that at which the horse is working on at home. If the horse is doing elementary work at home, then he is ready to compete at novice level in the arena.

Competing rarely helps to progress the horse's training other than to acclimatise him to strange circumstances and an arena, but it will certainly help the rider. It is helpful for any rider taking up dressage to get as much test experience as possible. If starting dressage with a good young horse rather than a schoolmaster, then it is best to try and beg or borrow rides on ponies or old horses. Compete wherever possible – even very low-key events help to establish a state of relaxed concentration rather than nervous paralysis and to learn the skills of arena craft.

AT HOME

PREPARING THE TEST

At home the rider should study the test that he is going to ride at the competition. If not working in an arena already, one should be laid out – buckets with the letters painted on them are sufficient for the markers, and the corners can be marked either with barrels or two poles to make the right angle. The horse needs to get used to the arena and working within its confines. Start with easy loosening work and progress towards some of the movements in the test. Practise one or two movements in a work session, find out the horse's weaknesses, and then carry out exercises to try and put right deficiencies.

When problems arise, it is rarely as helpful to go on practising a movement again and again, as to think about the problem, decide what is likely to be causing it, and then plan some remedial exercises. For example, if the horse is not lengthening his strides, then this is frequently due to him not having enough power from behind, not having sufficient impulsion, so more exercises should be done to help the engagement ie half halts, transitions, shoulder in (if he has reached this stage). For other common problems, see Chapter 8.

When the movements can be done reasonably well when practised individually, then they can be put together and the whole test ridden through once or twice. It is a mistake to do this too often as the horse tends to start anticipating what is going to happen.

TURNOUT

Dressage is an elegant sport, and turnout is very important. The horse needs a good grooming every day to help him feel well, to massage those muscles that are being used with such vigour, as well as to make him look good. For a show, his tail needs to be in good shape so in the weeks before ensure it is neatly pulled and frequently bandaged; if it is unpulled it can be plaited on the day.

The mane should have been pulled and on the day of the show plaited with cotton. Another style is to use elastic bands and then double up the plaits and secure them with white insulation tape.

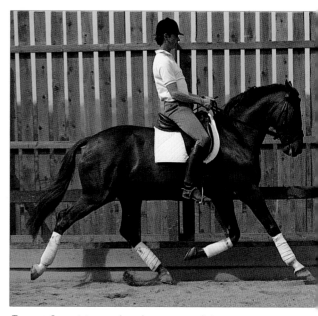

Turnout for training work at home or at clinics

A young Pony Club rider who is wearing, correctly, a hat with chinstrap, tie, tweed jacket, jodhpurs and jodhpur boots

Any white socks should be gleaming. They should be washed and if necessary whitened with chalk on the day of the show. The tail should also have been washed, and if it is white or light coloured, a little peroxide in the water helps to bring out this lightness. It is best to have washed the mane several days before the event as when freshly washed it is difficult to plait.

It is important that the horse does not get upset on his journey to the show, so before going to an actual event it is wise to take him on a number of trips in the horsebox, say, to a strange arena, for canters, best of all to a show itself where he need not compete but is just walked around to get used to the strange circumstances.

A list should be made of all the tack and equipment required on the day, and as much of this as possible put into the horsebox or trailer the night before. The tack should look very smart and have been well cleaned prior to the event.

One of the most important factors is to arrive in plenty of time. Plan well ahead to ensure that enough time is allowed for the journey, for preparing the horse at the show, and for the riding-in.

Above: A well dressed rider in a novice test – a tweed jacket is also acceptable

Right: Top hat and tailcoat for dressage at advanced level

PREPARING THE EQUIPMENT

THE HORSE Equipment needed at the show includes hay in a haynet for the return journey (it is best not to give hay on the way unless it is a very long journey); a feed if away at midday; water in a container; as well as a brush and fork to keep the horsebox clean.

The tack needed is a saddle, bridle, dressage numnah, and boots or bandages for the riding-in. If the test is to be done on grass then studs are needed, but most riders only put these in behind and use the pointed variety. If they are used in front, then they should be small, very pointed studs.

Appropriate rugs are needed such as a cooler/sweatshirt if the horse gets hot; warm, heavy rugs if the weather is cold; light summer sheets if it is hot. It is important to keep the horse at an even temperature, and when travelling check regularly to see that he is comfortable, neither sweating nor feeling very cold and in need of a change of rugs.

THE RIDER will need boots and breeches, although children on ponies can wear jodhpurs and jodhpur boots. The type of coat depends on the level of the event. All novice tests can be ridden in a tweed jacket with shirt and tie, although the fash-ion is growing to wear stocks instead of ties. At higher levels, black or navy jacket can be worn and at advanced levels, the tailcoat and top hat. Headgear at the lower levels varies, some wear bowler hats, the majority jockey hats and increasingly with chinstraps. Gloves must be worn and it is best to have these of a light colour (this is compulsory in England). Spurs can be worn at the lower levels, and in most countries from medium and above they are compulsory. A long dressage whip is an essential aid for the riding-in and the training of all but the most highly strung horses. Whips can be used in tests at most national levels.

THE SHOW

On the day of the show it is important to have allowed plenty of time, to have worked out a timetable and to keep checking your watch to make sure you are adhering to it.

In planning the timetable the following activities have to be taken into account. The Secretary has to be visited to get the numbers etc, the Steward has to be reported to, the horse has to be prepared — grooming, saddling him up, putting in the studs (if competing in a grass arena), putting on the brushing boots, and making the final touches to his appearance. Looking smart is a feature of dressage and that means the rider too who has to allow time for his own dressing up. Most important of all, time has to be set aside for the riding-in.

RIDING-IN

One of the most common excuses that riders have for not doing well in a test is that they either gave the horse too much work in the riding-in so that he was lazy and tired, or they did not give him sufficient so he was boiling over and explosive. It is very difficult to give the horse exactly the right amount of work. If, however, the horse is well established in his basics and therefore working well on the aids and submissive to the rider, he should do a good test even if he is a little fresh or a little tired. Also, if the work done in the riding-in is carefully thought through and planned, and is not a rather haphazard reaction to the situation on the day, the horse

Preparation for the event at the show. If you can, enlist the help of a friend

Riding-in at a Pony Club show. This rider is working closely with her trainer on the ground

should be ready to perform even if the test is a little earlier or later than planned.

The key to the riding-in is knowing your horse, mentally and physically. More time will be needed for the loosening up session at a show than it would at home, because the horse gets much more excited by the atmosphere. The time for the riding-in can only really be established after he has been to a few shows and his reactions to the atmosphere assessed.

It is better to allow too much time than too little. Then if he is working well and does not seem to need as much riding-in as anticipated, dismount, give him a little extra grooming and think about the test before returning to more riding-in. Taking a horse out twice for the riding-in is often a good solution for high-spirited horses who tend to get more and more tense as they do more and more work, and especially if their rider is getting more and more desperate as the time for the test approaches and the horse will not settle. For these horses it is a good idea to do some riding-in early on, either some lunge work, or some easy loosen-

ing up work. When they do settle, they can be put back in the box and given a shorter riding-in period before the test.

Lungeing is used by many riders as part of riding-in, particularly for horses who have excessively high spirits; these can then let off steam without endangering the rider or getting into a fight as to who is in control. It is also useful for stiff horses, as they can then loosen up without having the additional difficulty of carrying the weight of the rider.

The riding-in is important not just for the horse but also for the rider. Like horses, everybody tends to get more tense and excited at shows. Many riders would be embarrassed to do any loosening up exercises, but it is ridiculous to spend hours on loosening up the horse, but none on loosening up the rider. It is extremely beneficial to get into the saddle with relaxed muscles that have tone. For some riders this physical state might be an entirely natural one anyway, but others would benefit from a few exercises in the horsebox or trailer before they get on (see chapter 2).

It is also of value for the rider, when he first gets on the horse, to spend ten minutes or so at the walk on a free rein, thinking little about the horse but mainly about the riding position. Ensure that both those seat bones are in contact with the saddle, and that the weight is distributed evenly between them; that the legs can hang softly by the horse's side; that the back, neck and head are upright but relaxed; that the arms hang in a relaxed fashion, and that there is no pulling back with the hands.

Many riders, after they have done the initial riding-in in rising trot, cross their stirrups and do some work without them to help establish a deep, balanced position.

Much of the success in the arena depends on the rider's ability to establish relaxed concentration. It is important to aim for both these factors together and not to get so relaxed that all the riding-in time is spent chatting with friends and the concentration disappears, nor get so intense from trying hard that all the muscles tighten. The rider then cannot let go his muscles and feel what the horse is doing underneath him. There are today plenty of techniques to help sportsmen become more focused and able to make best use of their natural ability. For those who suffer from nerves there are plenty of books and seminars offering solutions.

The whole event must be treated as an exciting challenge, and the test an opportunity to try to get higher marks in each movement than on previous occasions. The test is not something to be frightened of, nor are the judges, and it is not something to try and get over and done with as quickly as possible.

Give the horse the opportunity to do his best possible work by finding an area for riding-in which is relatively secluded and with going which is as good as is available. Sometimes this is only a small area crowded with riders, and preparatory work is necessary for any horse to remain relaxed under these circumstances. Practise riding with other horses before going to a show so he is used to meeting them nearly head on, and having them pass

close to him. It is also important for the rider to become accustomed to this situation. Many get over-anxious and consequently upset their horses and make them more tense. Stick to the rules of that particular riding-in area, ie riding with the horse's left shoulder passing by the other horse's left shoulder, or as on the Continent, right shoulder to right shoulder. Ride confidently and positively and do not get overawed when famous riders head towards you.

Start with the loosening up work, and try to keep it along the same lines as that done at home. Get the horse going with rhythm, suppleness and accepting a contact with the legs, seat and hands. Contact is particularly difficult with high-spirited horses that are pulling in excitement. The natural reaction from the rider is to take the legs off his sides to try and stop the horse diving forward, and to use the hands to steady him. The problem is that much of this high spirited behaviour is done out of tension and in fact the confidence and security of leg contact is direly needed. It is crucial therefore to establish the leg contact and to get the horse to accept this without running away. If necessary start the work in small circles at the walk, keeping the leg quietly supporting the horse. The lazier horse is easier to cope with because it is much more natural for the rider to establish a leg contact with him.

If the horse jumps away every time the rider puts his leg on, then do a walk circle and ask the horse to move away from the inside leg in a leg yield (p96) so that he gets used to accepting the pressure of the leg. One of the easiest ways of doing this is on a large 20-metre circle. Just turn his head in slightly, and then ask him to move sideways in the walk, firstly in one direction, then change the rein onto another 15- or 20-metre circle and again turn him inwards; then ask him to move away from the inside leg to the outside rein. Get him used to the feel of the pressure of the inside leg, asking him to go away from it; also, keep supporting him with the outside leg.

When he starts to accept this pressure without jumping around, then go into working trot. Again be very careful to keep the legs closed lightly on his sides to give him support and help him to balance.

If he starts to run off, then do a transition to walk and ask again for small walk circles or a little leg yield or shoulder in. When the horse settles to accepting the leg again, make the transition once more into trot. Use plenty of half halts and transitions back to walk; keep him on a circle and avoid straight lines, and aim all the time towards establishing a very slow, steady tempo – but without taking the legs off the horse. He is only likely to settle when the legs are supporting him and if he tries to run away again then go back to exercises in the walk.

How the rider establishes the rhythm, the suppleness and the connection will depend greatly on his approach to dressage and the previous work at home. Most like to do a free walk on the long rein, then some rising trot, and as the rhythm becomes more pronounced, some canter work in the forward seat, or in a light basic position with little weight in the saddle. When the horse settles in this work, and lets go, then transitions can be made more frequently to increase the engagement and attention, and the amount of impulsion can be built up; but never ask for more than can be controlled without tension and explosions. Impulsion must be contained within the horse, not created one moment and lost the next as he takes off at speed.

With hot-blooded horses, the riding-in usually consists of no more than keeping them calm and trying to reduce the desire to go forward. There may be no need to create any more impulsion, especially at the easier levels of dressage. With the lazier horse, however, it may be necessary to generate energy, to concentrate on work that will encourage the engagement of the hindquarters, and the desire to go forward.

The important factor is to plan the work needed by your horse to bring him to the best possible state for the test.

Remember that the riding-in is not the occasion to train the horse. The test is merely a test of the training at home. If he is not very good at a movement, then there is no use at this stage in trying to make him better at it. He is very unlikely to improve on his performance at home, and in the arena very few horses go as well as they do at home. Aim to try and reproduce the type of work that is done at home.

When the basics – rhythm, suppleness, connection, impulsion and straightness – have been established to a reasonable degree, then start to try a few of the movements from the test. Do not wear him out by practising and re-practising what you are going to do in the arena, just aim to get him in the best possible state, mentally and physically, for the standard of work asked for in the test.

In all this riding-in work, it is helpful to have an assistant on the ground who can tell you if the horse is going straight, and warn you if the rhythm/tempo is getting a little too fast to show off his paces to the best advantage, if you are not sitting straight or are starting to pull backwards in the anxiety to prepare the horse for the test. This assistance does take some skill as it is very easy to upset a rider before going into the test. Only use as an assistant someone who has worked with you before, and who knows your horse and your approach; or somebody who is a real expert in dressage and has had plenty of practice at helping riders in the riding-in. It is a big mistake to change approaches and methods in the short time available before a test, so do not allow some well-meaning person to persuade you to try out a new technique just before going into the arena.

10

The Competitive Test

The test must be treated as an opportunity to show off, not something to be got through as fast as possible. It is amazing how many people go racing around the dressage arena at twice the speed they work at home when less nervous. This makes the movements look hurried and stiff, and the horse is more likely to lose his balance.

Try and divide the test up into the different movements. If something goes wrong in one of these movements, do not panic and throw away the rest of the test by losing relaxation and rhythm, but think of the next movement and prepare for that one thoroughly, correcting all that has gone wrong in the way of going as quickly as possible. Accept that there has been a hiccup, but get on with earning as many marks as possible in the following movements. It is very rare for anybody to go through a test without making mistakes, and it is quite possible to win prizes having made a fairly major mistake in one movement, as long as the rider is cool enough to re-organise and do good work again in the ensuing movements.

PREPARATION

The greatest weapon in test riding techniques is the half halt. Good riders use it constantly to help engage the horse, to prepare him for any movements, to warn him that something is about to happen, and to re-balance. Especially in the test these half halts should be barely perceptible, and only the expert should notice a straightening of the rider's back, the tiniest restraint with the hands before he slightly yields the pressure in the reins; but what should be more obvious is that the horse goes with greater self-carriage, greater collection and increased responsiveness. Practise using these half halts all the time at home so that they become second nature, and something you use before every corner, before every movement, and the moment anything starts to go wrong with the horse's way of going.

The half halt is used to warn the horse that something is about to happen, and is the first stage in preparing him for a new movement. This preparation is a crucial aid to test riding – with most of the great riders, three or four strides before they are about to do anything it is very easy to know what they are going to do. After warning the horse with the half halt, the horse is put in such a position that it will be easy for him to start the movement; it is not then necessary to rely purely on obedience.

For example, in a strike-off to the canter, a horse can be taught to go immediately into the canter on the correct leg as soon as the outside leg is taken back. But relying on this approach ie without preparing the horse for the movement, is not always successful; there are bound to be occasions when he is in the wrong bend, when he is running on or lacking impulsion, and one or more of these difficulties will make it very hard for him to get into the canter. If he is very obedient he will do so, but he is likely to tense up at the difficulty of having to cope with the handicaps of wrong bend etc.

The clever rider will ensure that he has the impulsion, the engagement, the correct flexion, and the correct balance before asking him to strike off – and then it will be very easy for him to do so, he can remain relaxed, trusting his rider and happy to obey him. Preparing in this way takes planning, thought and energy, but if you want to win rosettes it is one of the best ways of doing so.

Almost all tests start with a halt and a straight, square one with the horse on the bit gives an important first impression to the judge. This horse is just a little behind the vertical

ACCURACY

Accuracy is one of the most obvious aspects of good test riding. If the horse halts exactly at X, he will earn more points than the horse that halts three or four strides before or after it. Similarly the horse who is ridden in a true circle which is exactly of the diameter required, is likely to earn extra marks. Plan the figures very carefully, and work out which points in the arena to aim for so they can be ridden as accurately as possible. Especially in the more advanced tests, it is important that the movement is ridden from marker to marker, so when medium trot is asked for across the diagonal from H to F, then the medium trot begins at H and does not finish until F. Quite often horses are seen to establish the medium only two or three strides after H, and start to collect well before F. This is an effective means of throwing away marks. In the easier tests, transitions may be progressive so the horse is permitted to take two or three strides to establish the required pace.

WAY OF GOING

Many people think that accuracy is so important that they forfeit the horse's way of going in order to achieve it. For example, if a transition from canter to walk is asked for at E, they emphasise obedience and get the horse to walk exactly at E, but they do so regardless of whether it is at the expense of the basics. All too often rhythm and connection are lost and the horse starts to resist. Especially for riders who are ambitious to achieve more advanced levels of dressage, this is a great mistake in the training of the horse. The basics must remain a primary requirement. Especially with the young horse, it is much more important that he makes the transition on the bit, with the hinds engaged, and is fluent, than he does so exactly at the marker. Marks might be lost for inaccuracy, especially if the judge is relatively inexperienced and has a limited knowledge about training, but the good transition will help to further the horse's progress, the bad one will risk him becoming resistant and losing trust in his rider.

MEMORISE THE TEST

The rider can only ride the test confidently if he really knows it. Memorise at home, and if possible write it out, noting beside each movement the particular points needed for you and your horse to achieve the best possible results. That is, if your horse tends to hollow into the canter, then make a note that in the preparation you will need to work on achieving more softness and engagement in the preparation for the strike off to try and avoid this problem. On the day of the show, if you are riding many tests and will find it difficult to remember them all, it may help to have a caller to read out the test. This will give extra reassurance – but remember, many callers have made mistakes, lost their way, or had their voices drowned by an aeroplane flying overhead, so still learn the test yourself.

OVERALL IMPRESSION

Judges usually say they are not influenced by the overall impression, but it is very difficult not to give a few extra marks for combinations that look very smart and that have a confident air about them, and for riders who appear confident, and pat their horses.

POSITION

It is important that the competitor has a good position. There is a mark for this at the end and judges do tend to be more generous to those who are sympathetic poised and correct riders. Remember to sit straight and upright at all times, to keep the hands still (in England light gloves must be worn so that judges can note if hands are moving around), and keep the buttocks softly in the saddle and the legs close to the horse's sides. If there is any feeling of tension, then try a few deep breaths to help let go those rebellious, tense muscles.

ANALYSIS OF THE TEST

There is much to be learnt from each test. It is a good idea to put your reactions on paper as soon as possible after a test is completed. Make note of where errors were made, where the basics were lost, and what basics were not as established as required. Assess which basics need to be worked on and which movements need more practice.

Collect your judge's sheet, compare his/her reactions to the test, to your own. Make allowance for the

This horse is on his forehand and however accurate the test will lose marks in each movement that he puts so much weight on his shoulders and in the rider's reins

This rider has a good position and both he and the horse are smartly turned out to give a good overall impression

quality of the judge. Every comment from a leading and respected judge should be noted and worked on, but there are many judges who may have even less experience than the rider. One must be grateful to them for giving up their time to assess tests, but do not take every criticism they make as something to be worked on. The most important thing in training is to remain consistent, to decide on your principles, and to keep to them. The very good judges do work to consistent principles, but these take years and skill to acquire. Therefore do not try to adjust to advice given by every judge, as they may not be working to the same principles as you and your trainer.

As well as studying the judge's sheets and making your own notes, there is another very useful aid to improving test riding, and that is the video camera. Some competitors are fortunate enough to have their own, but at many shows there are professionals who do videos on request. Videos are a useful means of studying the good and bad points of a test and of assessing progress, between a test done earlier in the season with a later one. It is important to look at the test on the video two or three times in quick succession to really notice where the mistakes were made and where there are problems in the training.

Remember that it is impossible to do a perfect test. Nobody has ever achieved it. A few have earned the odd 10, but even with the great combinations this is very rare. Therefore be pleased with any good moments, with any improvements made on past tests. Do not get too dis-spirited when you cannot earn the top marks; there is enormous satisfaction to be gained in dressage simply from making progress, from finding solutions to problems. Just because it is impossible to find solutions to all the problems, it should not reduce the satisfaction to be gained when you do find a solution to a problem, however small, and know that it is your training which has led to any improvements. Dressage is intriguing because it consists of a series of never-ending challenges, and at times exhilarating when a solution leads to greater control and better realisation of the horse's natural talents.

The test is over and the pair leave the arena on a loose rein — now it is time for an analysis

RIDING THE TEST

To help the competitior understand what is needed to ride a good test, I have taken Novice No 30 as an example, and under each movement made notes as to some of the important points that he should be aware of and aiming towards.

I A enter at working trot. X halt. Salute. Proceed at working trot. C track left.

Do not rush into the arena when the bell goes. Give the horse any necessary preparations to make sure that his trot is balanced and rhythmical, that he is letting go, is on a good contact and has impulsion. If it is not as good as can be achieved, there is time for an extra circle, perhaps a transition or halt to increase the engagement, or a little shoulder in, or leg yielding to help him soften up and work straight. Do not keep the judge waiting too long, however, as after 60 seconds the horse is eliminated. Enter at a speed which makes it easy to halt, *ie* do not go too fast. Make sure the horse is straight, as the judge is looking directly at him. Start to prepare well before X, use those half halts to get the necessary engagement and attention. Ask for the halt which at this level can be progressive, *ie* two or three steps of walk can be shown if it makes the movement more fluent. Keep the legs on in a supporting aid, but as he is just about to come into the halt, ease the reins slightly so that he is able to stop square in front. Many riders pull on one rein more than the other, with the result that the foreleg on the side where the rein is pulling the hardest does not come so far forward.

Take the reins in one hand, and the stick if it is carried, and salute the judge. Take your time; make sure that the horse is still soft in the rein contact, perhaps play with the fingers a little to keep both softness and his attention, warn him that something is about to happen, and then ask him to proceed in working trot. Make sure he moves straight ahead, so look well out into the distance to help him achieve this. he will not lose marks if he takes one or two walk strides. The important point is to keep him on the bit and going forward into the hand.

After he has taken four or five trot strides, start to prepare him for the left turn ahead at C. Do not make the turn any sharper than he can manage while maintaining his rhythm. It is more difficult to go deeply into the corner, and this will not earn more marks in a Novice test, but any loss of rhythm will lose marks. Make sure he maintains a correct, slight flexion to the inside to the left as he goes round the turn.

2 E turn left; B track right.

A few strides before E, some more half halts, prepare a slight flexion to the left, and turn to the left just before E. Take care not to make the turn so sharp he cannot maintain the rhythm. Straighten him up and then before X start to warn him that he has another turn ahead, one or more half halts, then establish the slight right flexion and ask for the turn in sufficient time to be able to complete a smooth well defined turn. Keep thinking about and working on the rhythm, the balance, the engagement, the contact, the straightness, the impulsion.

Half halts to prepare the horse for the half circle, again preparation with that slight flexion, now to the right. Assess the half circle so that it is exactly 10 metres (just finishes on the centre line), and has a flowing smooth curve to it. Ensure he has enough collection to be able to do that 10 metre turn with balance. Maintain the rhythm, maintain the bend in the half circle. After D return to M on a straight line, ie he needs straightening up out of the slight right flexion. Again be very conscious of the rhythm and try to establish a good swinging trot. The working trot between M and H will give another opportunity to show off at his trot, so ensure that it is impulsive, swinging and soft.

In the corner before H, a series of half halts to help the engagement as the horse will only be able to lengthen his strides if he has the power to do so; the trot must therefore be made spring and impulsive through the corner. Leave the side of the arena at H but make sure he is straight and balanced before asking for the lengthening. Ask first with the legs and only when he starts to want to go and there is a slightly stronger contact in the hands, allow with the hands. Many riders just let the reins go and the horse falls onto the forehand and starts to run. It is important to keep up the same tempo – lengthening should not result in faster strides. The judges are looking only for the lengthening of the strides and will deduct marks for hurrying.

When the horse has shown a few lengthened strides, then start to collect him. Ask him to shorten up into the working trot, not by simply relaxing the aids for lengthening, but by a series of half halts using the legs and the seat to push him up into the hand so that the strides shorten with engagement. He should not be pulled back with the reins into the shorter strides. It is very easy for him to lose his balance after lengthening his strides and he will need help to re-establish a good, rhythmical, working trot.

Working trot F A K E is another chance to show off to the judge that your horse has a mark-earning rhythmical, springy trot.
Notes as for movement 2.

Notes as for movement 3.

Notes as for movement 4.

3 F D, half circle right, 10 metres diameter, returning to the track at M. M C H working trot.

4 H X F change the rein and progressively show some lengthened strides.

5 F A K E working trot, E turn right, B track left.

6 M G half circle left, 10 metres diameter returning to the track at F. F A K working trot.

7 K X M change the rein and progressively show some lengthened strides.

8 C medium walk, H X F, change the rein at a free walk on a long rein. F medium walk.

In the corner before C start to prepare the horse for the walk. Use a series of half halts so that he changes smoothly and with engagement into the walk and does not hollow and fall onto his forehand. When the walk is achieved, tactics will depend on your horse: if he is high spirited and tense, it will be necessary to remain very calm and quiet, but supportive with the legs, seat and hands. The voice cannot be used in the arena, but sit soft and heavy in the saddle and play gently with the fingers. If he is lazy, he will need aids from the leg and only a very gentle contact with the reins to encourage him to walk forward purposefully.

As he moves off the track at H to go across the diagonal, maintain the support of the legs and allow him to take the reins out of the hands. Ideally he should stretch forward and down and take long, free strides. He will only do this if the training has been correct. If he has not been using his muscles along his back and neck he will tend to remain in much the same outline and may even hollow his back and put his head in the air, demonstrating relief at no longer being held in place – if this is his tendency, then much more work needs to be done on the basics. In the arena, it helps if the contact is soft before he sets off across the diagonal. Before H ask for a tiny flexion to the right and a tiny flexion to the left, and then gently release the reins. Many riders do not allow their horses enough freedom to stretch down but keep their heads behind the vertical. Very occasionally the riders give the horse too much rein, flinging it away so it is a loose rein, not a free rein.

Before F, gradually start to take up the contact. With tense horses this is a difficult time and must be done especially tactfully. This movement can be practised at home turning the horse into a small circle if he feels as if he is about to jog.

9 At A, working canter right (transition may be progressive).

Just before A, ask for a little flexion to the right, start to prepare him for the transition. Make sure he is balanced so that he can strike off with ease onto the right lead. Aim to make the transition fluent and without loss of contact and rhythm, therefore one or two trot strides might be advisable.

10 E circle right 20 metres diameter, E H C M working canter.

Establish a good, bouncy, forward but not too fast canter. Maintain balance. Ensure the horse is not pulling too hard and use half halts as necessary. Before E half halt, prepare with a slight flexion to the right. Work on maintaining tempo, flexion, engagement and balance throughout the 20 metre circle.

11 M F Progressively show some lengthened strides. F working canter.

After C, start to prepare the horse for the lengthening of the strides. Two of the most important factors are that he has the engagement (the power) to do this, and that he is straight. Therefore use half halts, and think shoulder fore around the corner towards M. This will help to avoid the usual pitfall typical of most young horses, that they find it difficult to complete the turn and leave their quarters in, to end up going along the long side with their hind legs to the inside of the forelegs. Ask for a shoulder fore position before applying the aids for a lengthening. Use the leg and seat aids so that the horse takes a slightly stronger contact and then, as in the trot lengthening, allow with the hands. If the reins are given before the horse is asked with the seat and legs to increase the activity in the hindlegs, he will simply lengthen his head and neck and fall onto his forehand. Maintain the rhythm of the canter down the long side and keep the slight shoulder fore position. As F is approached, increase the half halts to re-establish the working canter. It is likely that the horse will find it difficult to balance after lengthening the strides, so use plenty of half halts and ensure that your position is upright.

When turning onto the diagonal, ensure the horse has sufficient engagement to keep balanced and that he is straight. As before, use plenty of half halts and think of shoulder fore positioning. Before X, use the half halts to get that extra engagement to warn him about the transition so that the transition can be smooth and fluent. Just after X start to prepare him for the left flexion and to gather enough impulsion for the transition into the canter.

Notes as for movement 10.

In the corner before F, use half halts to ensure the horse is balanced and engaged, and use shoulder fore positioning to ensure that he is straight. When he feels balanced and straight, gently push the hands and retake them in one smooth movement which should be over three to four strides of the canter. Keep the seat bones firmly in the saddle; do not lean forward as this will disturb his balance.

Notes as for movement 12.

Make sure that the trot is balanced and rhythmical. Use half halts as necessary. In the corner before A, start to prepare for the turn down the centre line, ask for that slight flexion to the right, ensure there is enough engagement. With the novice horse make the turn a smooth curve of a 10 metre half circle. Prepare for the halt as in movement 1. Salute the judge and hopefully give him a big smile as a sign that you have enjoyed the test because the horse gave you such a good ride. If he did, then the horse deserves a pat from his rider.

12 K X M change the rein, working trot at X, M working canter left.

13 M C H E working canter, E circle left 20 metres, E K A F working canter.

14 Between F and M, give and retake the reins.

15 M working canter, H S F change the rein, working trot at A.

16 F A working trot, A down centre line, X halt, salute.

BIBLIOGRAPHY

Boldt, Harry. *The Dressage Horse* (Edition Haberbeck, 1978)

Bürger, Udo. *The Way to Perfect Horsemanship* (J. A. Allen & Co Ltd, 1986)

Gallwey, W. Timothy. *Inner Game of Golf* (Jonathan Cape, 1979)

Klimke, Reiner. *Basic Training of the Young Horse* (J. A. Allen & Co Ltd, 1985)

Oliveira, Nuno. *Classical Principles of the Art of Training Horses* (Howley & Russell, 1983)

Oliveria, Nuno. *Reflections on Equestrian Art* (J. A. Allen & Co Ltd, 1976)

The Principles of Riding (Threshold Books, 1997). The official handbook of the German National Equestrian Federation

Regulations of the Fédération Équestre Internationale

Swift, Sally. *Centred Riding* (Kingswood Press, 1985)

Syer, John and Connolly, Christopher. *Sporting Body Mind* (Cambridge University Press, 1984)

Savoie, Jane. *That Winning Feeling* (J. A. Allen 1992)

INDEX

Page numbers in *italics* refer to photographs

Picture Acknowledgements

Photographs by Bob Langrish except the following:

pp35, 46, 58(top), 136 by Kevin Sparrow
pp6, 7, 10, 16, 17, 26, 27, 31, 37, 41, 42, 56, 58(btm), 59, 60, 67, 70, 72, 87, 88, 97(left), 104, 105(left), 110, 113, 114–15, 117, 119(top), 120, 121, 127, 129, 132, 133, 140(btm), 143, 151(top), 152–3 from the author's collection

Line artworks by Maggie Raynor